SELF-DIRECTED LEARNING IN
COUNSELLOR TRAINING

COUNSELLOR TRAINER AND SUPERVISOR SERIES

SELF-DIRECTED LEARNING IN COUNSELLOR TRAINING

Mary Charleton

CASSELL

Cassell
Wellington House
125 Strand
London WC2R 0BB

127 West 24th Street
New York
NY 10011

First published 1996

British Library Cataloguing-in-Publication Data
A catalogue record for this book is available from the British Library.

ISBN 0-304-32941-X (hardback)
    0-304-32943-6 (paperback)

Library of Congress Cataloging-in-Publication Data
Charleton, Mary.
    Self-directed learning in counsellor training/Mary Charleton.
        p.   cm. — (Counsellor trainer and supervisor series)
    Includes bibliographical references and index.
    ISBN 0-304-32941-X (hardback). — ISBN 0-304-32943-6 (pbk.)
    1. Counselors—Training of.   2. Counseling—Study and teaching.
I. Title.   II. Series.
BF637.C6C374   1996
361.3'23'0715—dc20   96–500
                                                                   CIP

Typeset by Action Typesetting Limited, Gloucester
Printed and bound in Great Britain by
Biddles Ltd, Guildford and King's Lynn

Contents

Foreword

I first trained as a counsellor in 1975. Since that time interest in counselling in Britain has mushroomed. For example, membership of the British Association for Counselling (BAC) continues to grow and training courses in counselling are cropping up everywhere. Fortunately, this growth in the development of counselling in Britain has been paralleled by an increasing concern that counsellors need to be properly trained and their work professionally supervised. The Counsellor Trainer and Supervisor series is designed to reflect this developing interest in the training and supervision of counsellors. It is the first series in Britain devoted to these two important and related professional activities and seeks to provide a forum for leading counsellor trainers and supervisors to share their experience with their novice and experienced colleagues.

Mary Charleton has been at the forefront of the self-directed learning approach to counsellor training for many years. In this volume, she draws on her vast experience to illustrate the issues that need to be considered when planning, establishing and running a counsellor training course based on self-directed learning principles. Trainers wishing to run such a course will find much of value within these pages. This book will also stimulate trainers who run courses not founded on these principles and challenge them to re-evaluate their view of the nature of counsellor training.

Windy Dryden

Preface

The purpose of this book is to explore the meaning of self-directed learning and its application in the training of counsellors. The book is divided into two parts. Part One looks at the rationale, major dilemmas and how to deal with them. Part Two focuses on how to put self-direction into action in training, and details the necessary tasks and the skills that go with them.

The book starts by looking at the way most people experience learning in traditional educational institutions. It describes how the self-directed model of counsellor training sets out to support the autonomy of the learner. The link is made between this type of training and a practitioner who supports her clients' power and autonomy. A main concern is to demonstrate that a training in counselling can make use of the medium of training in order to emphasize the content.

The central issues in self-directed learning are examined. There is a discussion of power and authority, dealing with such topics as bias and prejudice, creating a safe environment, institutional support, how the process can go wrong and what to do. A developmental model is offered and described in some detail together with exercises and methods of facilitating. The model draws on the author's experience running counselling courses at South West London and Southwark Colleges.

The working of the large group, of central importance for courses using self-directed learning, is described to show how it provides immediate experience of psychological methods of defence, interpersonal skills, the influence of psycho-dynamic processes and the skills of working with and within an organization.

The book defines and clarifies the notion of self-direction and offers suggestions about creating a useful learning environment and having strategies for safeguarding it. Suggestions are made about how to reinforce the principles and deal with the inevitable resistance.

Acknowledgements

I would like to express my appreciation of all the students and staff I knew at South West London and Southwark Colleges. I am still working with the issues raised and the insights gained.

In particular I would like to thank the following, who filled in questionnaires and in other ways gave freely of their time and knowledge: Caro Bailey, Celestine Chakravarty-Agbo, Sue Condon, Shelley Gurney, Suzanna Hobkirk, Linda Horsfall, Melanie Lockett, Shirley Margerison, Geraldine Rose, Ernest Woollett.

This book would not have been written without the help and constructive criticism of my two editors, Windy Dryden and Maria Stasiak.

I would also like to acknowledge my husband's unfailing support and encouragement and the interest, patience and impatience of my friends.

Finally, I would like to thank my supervisor, Dennis Hyde, for his support, ideas and attentiveness.

Patanjali declares that the true secret of evolution is the manifestation of the perfection which is already in every being; that this perfection has been barred and the infinite tide behind is struggling to express itself. Even when all competition has ceased this perfect nature behind will make us go forward until everyone has become perfect.

Patanjali, *c.* 400 BC

ONE
Introduction

As counselling trainers we expect the learner to have the greatest possible control over what she learns and how she learns it. We take the position that the learner can function well if she is asked to be aware of her goals in learning and to direct herself towards them, using the trainer as a guide. By taking this position we are expressing our faith in the essential goodness and wisdom of the individual and her capacity for change and growth.

The strongest argument that can be made for self-directed learning in counsellor training is that it mirrors the counselling process by working to giving as much control as possible to the user of the service. Students on counselling courses using self-directed learning are assumed to be knowledgeable, skilful and creative. It is from this standpoint that the method can be made operational.

An inseparable part of being self-directing is that of creating the milieu where this can occur. This immediately involves working successfully with others. People discover that being self-directing necessitates working collaboratively. This widens the focus from the self to the self in contact with others. Learning to be with other people in a new more open way, to trust those relationships and use them positively is the matrix of learning and growth.

On courses using this method students create an organization for learning.

They are encouraged to take great interest in the process of learning, in the way learning happens. They notice the effect of different interventions and discover how their reactions enhance or inhibit learning.

WHAT IS LEARNING?

When we learn well we follow an interior authority. We acquire a new behaviour pattern which helps us change the way we behave or think. We create our own world, retaining hope and a sense of wonder. Through experience and useful instruction we gain skills and knowledge which enable us to manage our lives in the world as it is and to go on changing and adapting our environment to suit ourselves and those around us.

This is a very positive definition of learning. It is clear also that people often learn solely in order to pass exams, often acquire skills that are harmful to themselves and others, and often feel they have to stop being fully human in order to learn.

HOW WE LEARN

We all have some theory or idea about how learning happens. Children are rewarded or punished in particular ways on the understanding that this will encourage them to behave in a socially approved way. The key issue for the individual is to know how she learns.

Kolb's learning cycle (Figure 1.1) provides a good model for learning from experience. An individual can learn by waiting for something to happen to her and then reflecting on that experience; she can also actively seek experience from which she can learn. The second stage involves allowing time and space to reflect and review the learning experience. After the review, it is possible to reach the third stage and form a conclusion. The final stage is to plan future action on the basis of the conclusion.

It is uncommon for people to be effective at all of these stages. Some people are stronger in the more active phases at the beginning and end of the cycle than at reflection and review. Sometimes the skills of the reflective stages are de-emphasized in favour of the more active phases. It is helpful to be able to use the skills involved in all four stages, to be able to

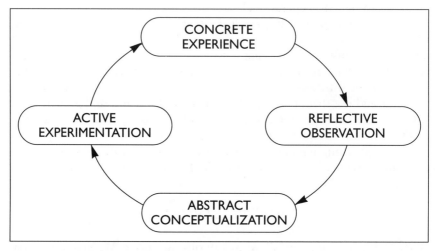

Figure 1.1 The experiential learning cycle

act, reflect, make decisions and reach conclusions as well as be able to plan future actions. Students can be encouraged to redraw Kolb's diagram to fit their own learning story.

If the learner understands her learning style she will have the confidence to insist on conditions that are right for her. She will also be able to change her learning style if she wishes. The student's awareness of her personal style and abilities is a good basis for further learning. For example, if she knows that she is a reflective learner she can ensure that she makes use of this ability and also ensure that she learns to strengthen the areas in which she is weaker. Traditional ways of learning do not always allow for these differences or allow the learner to learn more about how to learn.

TRADITIONAL WAYS OF LEARNING AND OBSTACLES TO EFFECTIVE LEARNING

Our first learning experiences happen within our families. Our attitudes towards those in authority and to learning in general are formed by the way in which our parents touch, speak, hear and correct us. Their response to the way we explore and understand the world are key to our definition of ourselves as learners. If their responses to our exploration are negative or punitive, we may begin to doubt ourselves and distrust our experience.

Our next set of associations to the word learning is likely to be connected with school, the classroom and most important of all, the teacher. She or he is usually of immense importance and often we think of ourselves as going to school to take in knowledge from the teacher. We observe, read and memorize while the teacher sets objectives, evaluates and assesses. Learning is thought to be an activity confined to the classroom and – to a large extent – concerned with acquiring abstract ideas and concepts. It is mostly related to an academic subject and the teacher tells the child what she knows about the subject. It can seem very separate from doing and from solving the problems of ordinary life. Kolb's learning cycle attempts to bring learning about ideas and practical problem-solving together. Developments in NVQs, especially the identification of core skills, also challenge traditional ideas.

In traditional education students are still assumed to need knowledge to be given to them and the way in which this is done is decided by someone other than the learner. This situation may not provide for differences in individual receptivity and ways of processing information. The learner is not encouraged to follow her own lead and learn at her own pace. The relationship between teacher and learner is not examined and the learner may come to accept a powerless position. Assumptions and presumptions are often made about what should be done. The assumptions are not often made explicitly available or democratically tested and adapted so that the individual learner can find her own route.

The recognition that people naturally and inevitably learn in different ways needs to be combined with the awareness that many of us have been blocked in our understanding because of previous hurtful or damaging learning experiences. Frequently the pain and hurt resulting from these experiences have not been recognized, often even by the sufferer herself. Where the suffering is not expressed, it is not possible to come to a resolution or understanding and move forward. This hidden distress can hamper subsequent learning. Harvey Jackins and John Heron have written extensively about the ways in which our unexpressed distress occludes our intelligence (Jackins, 1973; Heron, 1977).

SELF-DIRECTED LEARNING – WHAT IS IT?

Self-directed learning is a method of learning in which students set their own objectives and gain the knowledge and skills they require. Self-directed learning places the power and responsibility in the hands of the learner. It aims to give the learner as much control as possible over the *what* and the *how* of learning. The teacher or staff member becomes a facilitator who ensures that the conditions for effective learning exist. She watches over the process of learning and makes comments which are intended to help the learner understand her way of working. The learner is expected to become aware of her personal and professional aims and to arrive at goals which support these aims.

The learner can use her experience to generate rules and principles which can guide her in the next experience. She will in turn modify the rules and principles as a result of that experience. Rather than sitting with her mouth open to receive the worm of knowledge she becomes an explorer, an experimenter, a reflecter and a planner.

Inherent in self-directed learning is the assumption that the student can become an expert on herself and her wants and needs. She will know more than the course provider about what she should learn. There is a further assumption that she will have at least an implicit understanding of how she learns best. Self-directed learning takes account of the whole human organism and assumes that people can learn through many aspects of their being: through seeing, tasting, touching, hearing, smelling, loving and hating as well as through their considerable intellectual potential.

As a group of self-directing learners, students facilitate each other's learning and form a peer learning community. They help each other construct a plan which will help them reach their goals. They make their skills and talents available to others in a variety of ways, from informal group discussion and skill-swapping to more formal project work and supportive role play. They arrive at ways of monitoring and evaluating their learning. They construct methods of self and peer assessing. They learn a great deal about themselves and their methods of defence through observation, instruction and experiential learning in the large group. Experiential learning refers to the kind of learning that happens when a young child accidentally touches an electric fire and gets burned, or discovers that two pence plus two pence equals four pence. She may have previously been told these things and accepted them cognitively. She learns experientially when she is personally involved in that learning; when it makes a difference to her as a person and to her behaviour; when she notices and evaluates that difference; and when she is organismically involved in what is happening. She will use her intuition and imagination as well as her more linear, logical left-brain functions. As the students learn about counselling they also learn to plan and to govern themselves as a community; they set up student-run workshops and other projects to support and illuminate their learning; they produce a portfolio of work; they plan and set up a timetable based on needs and resources and they take part in individual and group supervision. They direct that learning and are closely involved in it. That involvement is personal and uses their senses, imagination, emotions and intellect.

In a more conventional system the power to decide what is to be learned and how well it is being learned is external to the learner. In most cases she is the recipient of information that others believe she needs. The goals are set before the course starts and the methods of monitoring and assessment are controlled by external criteria.

HISTORICAL AND THEORETICAL UNDERPINNINGS

Many of the great educational theorists, for example, Rousseau, Montessori, Paulo Freire, John Dewey and A. S. Neill, held ideas that were congruent with a learner-directed approach. They all believed in the individual's ability to learn well from experience. They were of the opinion that many formal educational and societal norms tended to cramp and harm individual development and the ability to learn, and wanted to find ways for the individual to be free to learn and develop according to her current needs; they would also have approved supporting the individual to reflect, review and prioritize her learning needs.

The first person to apply a learner-directed approach systematically to the training of counsellors and therapists was Carl Rogers. He believed in encouraging and enhancing experiential learning and in trusting the student to find a direction and decide on priorities. His Person-centred approach has had a profound effect on counselling and counsellor training. Rogers' early training was psycho-dynamic; but he always remained open to other ideas, maintaining a lively, pragmatic interest in what worked and engaging in extensive research on his evolving methods. Through careful observation and monitoring of clients' behaviour, and beginning after a time to take his lead from the client, Rogers came eventually to the view that the more he could be truly himself with another person – be they student, client, or friend – the more helpful and real he could be for that person and the more potential for growth there would be for both parties.

He believed that people had within them a basically positive direction and that, like plants, they would flourish if given the essential conditions for growth: warmth, empathy and genuineness.

This realization had implications for the method of therapy he evolved and for the approach to be used in training people in his methods. He and people influenced by him found it impossible to continue taking the position of 'expert' on what other people needed to do or learn.

Rogers' theories grew out of the Romantic tradition, particularly as represented by thinkers such as Rousseau, Froebel and Pestalozzi. Freedom of expression, the importance of the individual and the goodness of the individual are central tenets. Rogers placed a great deal of importance on people's subjective experience. The major emphasis of his work consisted in helping individuals discover their feelings and work from them. These ideas are in sympathy with Gestalt theories of perception and an Existential emphasis on immediacy and the primacy of present experiencing.

The course at South West London College pioneered the use of self-directed learning in counselling training in this country, and was influenced also by John Heron's work on peer learning communities at Surrey University; it included self and peer assessment as the logical outcome of an authentically self-directed approach. The essential single concept that underlines the use of self-directed learning in counselling training is that it mirrors the counselling process by enhancing and increasing the autonomy of the learner just as the counsellor works to strengthen that of the client.

Facilitating self-directed learning involves helping people to contact their feelings fully, stay in touch with what they are experiencing at any given moment and use their subjectivity effectively rather than being at the mercy of it.

HOW DOES SELF-DIRECTED LEARNING WORK?

If the learner is to direct herself she will need to discover a way of learning that suits her. This will involve trying a number of different approaches and experiencing success and failure without undue praise or blame. Some people will fear success as much as failure. They may be unsure about how to handle the responsibility that accompanies success and/or they may fear envy from those who do not achieve as easily. There must be time to feel the feelings that accompany success or failure and time to analyse and learn from such experiences. Clear immediate feedback is one of the most helpful ways of encouraging both experiential and self-directed learning.

Students are encouraged to focus on their experience as it happens. By noticing their reactions to events and being open about these and being available to feedback from peers they will come to an understanding about how the helping process works.

Students use all the conventional resources, such as tape recorders, video cameras, journals and books, but most importantly they work with their experience as learners and human beings. Consequently rooms filled with learners are lively places. There is a buzz of energy, laughter, tears, love and hate. All kinds of strong emotions are evoked as people remember previous learning experiences when childish curiosity had too often been squashed or at worst punished. They differentiate previous unhappy learning experiences from what is occurring in the present. In this setting as 'student teachers' they are respected as learners and as people who can help others learn.

This process allows for a new kind of relationship with the subject being studied. People accept authority from within themselves and from their personal belief systems. This is intensely relevant to the work they are being trained to do. They follow an inner direction rather than trying to adapt themselves, their experience and their belief system to an imposed model. They seek actively to learn and to decide their priorities. No longer expected to be a passive recipient in a process that affects them profoundly, they are encouraged to be proactive.

This emphasis on people working with whatever they need to learn and deciding how they want to learn it is the essence of self-directed learning. It implies any number of different ways of learning: for example, workshops, seminars, reading, role play, skills practice, T groups, video and audio recording and observation of counselling using two-way mirrors. It does not exclude lectures or deadlines but it does imply negotiation over these. There is a respect for the self and the uniqueness of the individual learner. She will be encouraged to be in touch with that self and her wants and needs at any particular time and to use that, rather than a desire to please others, as a base for learning.

For example, a student who is working to improve the ways she deals with angry people can be encouraged to notice if the norms of the learning community and the timetable that is being formed are helpful to her learning. If they are not and she feels angry about this, she can be encouraged to notice how she is responding to her feelings. She may be putting a great deal of energy into suppressing them, or she may be expressing them in a way that is unhelpful to her. The staff can encourage her to work towards a timetable that will take her learning needs into account.

The student will come to understand more about how she absorbs information, gains skills and comprehends and acquires knowledge. The self-directed learning course is likely to offer workshops on learning styles, on creativity, on using art to discover hidden needs, and on how to monitor progress in learning about counselling.

The aim will be to set up a system of learning focused on the needs of the individual rather than to ask the person to suppress her needs in order to fit in with an externally created system. A student who does not learn well from books can ensure that she receives new information in other ways, for example, tapes, dramatization, visiting other students' workplaces and in other ways that she will be able to suggest for herself. However, in the early stages it usually takes a staff member to suggest that different ways are possible. People do not come naturally or easily to this way of working.

WHAT HAPPENS IN SELF-DIRECTED LEARNING?

The students work in a co-operative group. They come together to share responsibility for the learning that is done. They take responsibility for what and how they learn and are also committed to helping others learn. They are prepared to share their own skills and knowledge as well as to benefit from the experience, skills and knowledge of their peers.

They must be shown how to do this and supported by experienced facilitators. Their assumptions about leadership will be challenged and they will be encouraged to develop their abilities to lead and to follow others in a conscious way which will increase their knowledge and skills.

One aim is to create a system where there is a fluid exchange between the roles of teacher and learner. Through creating their own organization for learning the students learn to adapt their environment so that it is facilitative to their needs at the time.

WHAT ARE ITS BENEFITS?

One person who had always been very successful academically spoke about what self-directed learning meant to her:

> Working in this way gave me a greater sense of process, of working with the whole of me. I did not have to cut off part of me in order to be an intelligent human being. I could use the whole of me. There were a whole lot of new things to do and learn and a new way to learn it all, involving skills and talents I did not know I had, e.g. drawing, visualizing, using my hunches, respecting my reaction to present events.

In a different situation, another former student who was dyslexic and had not always achieved her potential in the past found that the emphasis on action, skills training and experiential learning gave her the chance to excel publicly, to feel and sense her intelligence and communicate that to others.

It is not unusual for people to describe themselves as having changed their lives after taking part in a course involving self-directed learning. They become active in planning and organizing their lives as well as their learning and frequently make extensive and profound changes in the direction of more authentic living.

For example, a woman student may find the strength to move out of an unsatisfactory relationship, saying of the course 'It changed my life' – shorthand for 'I changed my life when I found the tools'.

As students gain an experience of systems and ideas that can be adapted to human need they will be more likely, as citizens of a wider world, to question and recreate their environment rather than passively accepting it. Their belief system changes. They realize that they can have more power and influence in the world than they hitherto thought was possible. They learn this not through being told it, but by being available to their own experience.

Students learn not only to work collaboratively but to communicate with one another in a new way. They will be expressing needs and wants that affect them deeply rather than what they have been taught in the past or what they think they are expected to say. This spontaneous approach affects the medium for learning, which becomes more stimulating and less predictable. By exploring and encouraging the peer relationship and the need for collaboration in learning, people relate to each other at unusual depth and find out a great deal about other people and themselves. Events are perceived freshly and are ascribed their present meaning rather than seen always in terms of personal history. A staff member can be seen as a person rather than as an embodiment of a past headmistress. The individual becomes part of a process rather than a passive recipient of a product. She can recognize the process and, if necessary, change it. She is in touch with her feelings rather than being at the mercy of them.

The student is motivated to learn and develop by being with others who want to do the same. She gains hope and the belief that change is possible. That, in turn, is communicated to clients, not in so many words but in the very nature of the experience that is offered.

This chapter sets the scene and defines self-directed and experiential learning. In Chapter 2 there is a consideration of the particular relevance of self-directed learning to counselling. Major features such as feedback, monitoring, evaluation and assessment are looked at. There is also a discussion of the function of workshops and the use of the portfolio.

PART ONE

The rationale for a
self-directed approach
to counsellor training

*Issues, challenges, dilemmas and their
management*

Two
Self-directed learning and counselling

This chapter examines the particular suitability of self-directed learning for counsellor training. It demonstrates how a course using a self-directed learning model operates through the process of:

- Feedback
- Self- and peer-monitoring
- Evaluation
- Assessment
- Constructing a portfolio
- Choosing, taking part in and helping to run workshops.

Examples are given of practical exercises that could be done with students. There is a discussion of the way workshops function, and of the use of the portfolio in self-directed learning and self and peer assessment.

Self-directed learning has a particular applicability to counselling. In self-directed learning the learner is trusted to look after herself and is looked upon as a good, trustworthy organism, able to meet her own needs once she is clear what these are. In counselling we take great care to respect and enhance the autonomy of the client; we do not make decisions for her or tell her what to do. We are concerned to help her learn about herself and make her own good decisions. We want her to feel safe and yet challenged enough to take risks to learn more. We want a training course to give the students an opportunity to grow and change at their own rate and in a direction that they choose. The staff are there to make sure that good conditions for learning exist, not to direct the students or decide what they should learn. They encourage them to prioritize goals and take steps to meet them.

Counsellors encourage their clients to become self-actualizing, in other words, to fulfil their potential for personal growth and development. They do this by helping them to perceive and fulfil their needs. Trainee counsellors on a self-directed training are given the same encouragement in relation to their learning. They are asked to monitor continually whether or not what they are learning is meeting their personal and professional needs.

At the start of the course the students work in a large group to compose a timetable. As they do this, they realize that they need to find ways of working together that will enhance rather than impede their progress. They will need to encourage each other, and sometimes to let each other know that particular interventions can be hurtful or obstructive. They will want to understand more about group dynamics and how to operate in small and large groups. They will need to delegate certain functions to small groups, and learn how to give these groups a useful brief and offer them helpful feedback and evaluation at the end. In general, students at the start of a course do not know how to do this and clumsy judgements can be made, with unhelpful consequences. Thus they need to work hard at learning how to give feedback, and at finding ways to monitor, evaluate and assess. The following descriptions of these four tasks are intended to provide a way of working gradually towards a full-scale appraisal of each other's progress (as well as being a good way for professionals to work together to improve and safeguard standards).

These four tasks are intrinsic to the processes of skill building and becoming a self-directing human being. They are a major feature in self-directed learning and are essential tools for the reflective practitioner throughout her professional life. On a training course of this kind, these tasks are chiefly formally carried out in workshops and in connection with the portfolio. In a learning organization initiatives towards continuous feedback, monitoring, evaluation and assessment need to be carried out on the first day and continue at each developmental stage of self-directed learning, in order to help students assess their progress and revise their learning plans.

The self-directing practitioner will want to know how to monitor, evaluate and assess herself rather than waiting for an external judgement. This is in keeping with what she encourages her client to do: to monitor her wants and needs as counselling progresses and assess whether or not these are being met.

A good way to help a student to monitor her own progress and to self assess well is to offer her a range of strategies for knowing her practice and putting it in a context. A useful way to start is with feedback.

FEEDBACK

In the early stages of the course before they know each other well or have written their portfolios, students must decide when, where and how they can give each other access to their work so that they can give and get feedback.

Feedback is a description of what is seen, heard and felt. It should be given without judgement or evaluation or assessment. It should be given with the intention of benefiting the receiver and should not be the long-awaited opportunity for the giver to express difficult feelings. It should be done in a professional way, under the right circumstances and with a clear contract which states limits and boundaries. The giver and receiver should decide together what the feedback should concern, how long it should go on for, whether the receiver wants any particular support, whether or not it should be written and whether or not it is confidential. Students will want to practise giving feedback and may wish to have a workshop which teaches them to give feedback well.

The climate and culture of a course should encourage helpful feedback. Being able to step to one side of prejudices and the emotional baggage left by personal problems and anxieties is a difficult but necessary part of giving helpful feedback. Feedback is only helpful when it is a response to what is happening *now*.

The following minimal counselling skills are of use in helping students pay enough attention to give useful feedback:

- attending and listening
- offering warmth, genuineness and empathy
- refraining from offering unhelpful interventions
- not interrupting or diverting attention away from the central issue
- not being absorbed in their own problems or concerns
- being alive to issues that concern minority groups.

Students should ask for feedback, rather than have it thrust upon them. Before people ask for, or receive, feedback they should decide what they want feedback on and from whom they would like to receive it. Do they want feedback on the *way they work* with another person or on *what they achieve* as a counsellor?

Feedback should be accurate and relevant. It should be given in small manageable units which enable students to understand and recognize something about their counselling style. For example, if they are told that they have asked four questions in six minutes they may conclude that they would like to find other ways of encouraging their clients to talk. They may for instance decide to ask fewer questions and make more reflections.

Feedback should convey the message that change is possible and within the reach and control of the learner.

Students will have to be taught to distinguish the various elements in any communication in order to know the difference between making a diagnosis, offering a theory or using a particular intervention or strategy, and feedback, which does not include any of these. It allows the receiver to gain more information about how she is performing in, for example, a counselling session. This does not mean an evaluation but simply how she is seen and heard.

The aim of feedback is to help people become more aware of how others perceive them. It constitutes the link between the self and others. When given well, with the right intention and with integrity, it creates a relationship of unusual honesty and closeness. It is an unconventional form of communication and very challenging of conventional norms. People feel safe to say some of the things that are often left unsaid and consequently cope more readily with unsocial aspects of themselves and others.

A useful model for giving non-judgemental feedback is that designed by Virginia Satir (Satir, 1972). She distinguishes between levelling (saying what is happening and how you feel about it) and four other types of communication: blaming, distracting, computing (generalizing or over-intellectualizing) and placating. People often have a predominant way of communicating, which they learned within their families and have used constantly ever since. For example, they may tend to blame a great deal because this happened to them as children. Blaming is not a stance from which to give helpful feedback and is likely to flip an unprepared student into a placating style of response. The student is then on the defensive and is not able to educate herself by concentrating on the content of the feedback. However, if the course community has become a good medium for learning, then the student can be accepted and valued as a human being even if she has not performed well as a counsellor. Students generally learn to level with each other and come to see that the other four methods are usually used as a defence and can be dispensed with. They realize that they have a right to refuse feedback that is not given competently.

It will always be important for the person giving feedback to ask herself the following questions:

- Is this person ready to hear what I would like to tell her?
- Is what I have to tell her for her benefit or mine?
- Will this person be able to change in the light of the feedback I give her?
- Do I give more positive or more negative feedback?
- How does this reflect on me as a person?

Students will normally welcome and make use of well-timed feedback competently given. One student used feedback in the following way:

> In the third year I chose to work in a triad looking at my practice, working directly on counselling skills, giving feedback verbally and using tape and video material. This was instead of the more usual support group. This was invaluable in developing and focusing on my

skills as a counsellor. The two people I chose were people I felt safe with and trusted that they would give me honest yet gently given feedback that would help me grow.

I think the honesty and extent that people were able to give constructive feedback helped me in my ability to look at myself and direct my learning.

A number of models exist which break counselling skills down into smaller units or micro skills. These can be used in practice sessions so that the students receive feedback from as many different sources as possible concerning the skills that they most often use. A micro skills model, which offers a framework for distinguishing different interactive skills, is an important aid to feedback (see p. 20 for a possible model).

Some students will at first find it very difficult to give useful feedback. This may be due to fear of hurting another person, to a lack of clarity on what counselling is, or to emotional blockages or emotional difficulties within themselves. As they become aware of these things they will usually ask for personal development groups and workshops on giving feedback. Staff may also suggest these things.

Creating an environment where it is safe to give useful feedback is the key to the successful organization of a community of learners. It helps people judge where they are in their hierarchy of learning needs. The encouragement of competent feedback is a major feature in transforming the large group of students so that it becomes an organization in which its members learn and offer learning opportunities to others.

Effectively given feedback helps people learn more about themselves and other people. Students will then want to consider the significance of this for their professional practice. They will want to be able to give useful well-timed feedback to clients. They will want to think about what to do with their increased self-awareness and self-knowledge. They will want to use this to direct their learning in ways that are useful to them. They will now have stronger ideas for future workshops. They will want help and guidance to increase their strengths and handle weak points.

SELF AND PEER MONITORING

Monitoring involves seeing someone work as a counsellor, noticing what skills they use and thinking about their implication for effective counselling. Monitoring helps the trainee counsellor look at the skills and knowledge she already has and decide what else she wants to learn. People can also be monitored to help them notice whether or not they are being self-directing. Students can sometimes make quite self-denigratory statements. For example, 'I am not very good at reflecting' or 'I don't make good summaries'. A staff member will challenge this kind of attitude by asking the student to think about how she will handle this difficulty. She may ask:

- What do you need to learn?
- How do you want to learn it?
- How will you know that you have learned it?
- Are you getting your needs met on this course?

The staff member supports the student's self-direction. She does not rescue the student or organize her learning for her. Instead she encourages the student to notice whether or not she is getting what she wants from the course and encourages her to think concretely about her learning needs and to make sure she gets them met.

What needs to be monitored?

Skills and knowledge need to be monitored to ensure that these are adequate and appropriate to the students' counselling work. Specially constructed exercises enable them to look at the skills they use most frequently and to become aware of which other skills are available to them. Early monitoring enables students to notice what use they have made of their learning plan and whether or not it needs altering in the light of their own and other people's perceptions and comments. Monitoring can also help them notice whether or not they are being self-directing.

An effective practitioner should be constantly monitoring her work and making that work available to monitoring and feedback from others. On a self-directed learning course monitoring is one of the early building blocks for self and peer assessment. People start by noticing the skills they and others use and wanting to improve on these. In the final stage they will have the task of deciding whether or not they and their peers are good enough to qualify as effective counsellors. Becoming effective at monitoring affords useful practice at noticing and distinguishing skills and provides a platform for later evaluating and assessing.

Students realize that they need to be taught how to monitor their work and at an early stage will generally ask for workshops that enable them to learn how to do this.

For instance, students can be asked to brainstorm what they believe are the important counselling skills. These can be listed and then, during a practice session, observers can record beside the list of skills how often each is used. The list is then handed, without judgement, to the person taking the role of counsellor. She may be surprised at the number of times she has used a particular intervention or at how little she has used another. This should make her more aware of her counselling style and of which of her interventions are inhibiting or facilitating. She can also be encouraged to notice how powerful or powerless she feels in relation to receiving feedback and be asked what she wants to do for herself in this regard. It is likely that she will want to revise her learning plan in the light of the feedback and monitoring she receives.

How can students monitor their work?

Monitoring can be done very effectively in small groups of between six to ten people. In the early stages people can, as suggested above, brainstorm a list of basic skills, for example attending, listening, demonstrating empathy, summarizing and focusing. The group can then divide into small subgroups, with different students taking the parts of counsellor, client and observer(s) (the client material should preferably be real rather than acted), and with the counsellor being monitored in accordance with the agreed list of skills. Later, as students become more experienced and knowledgeable, they can bring in written material and audio and video recordings of their work. As people practise monitoring and become better at it these live recordings become immensely stimulating and inspiring. People gain ideas about how to work and also increase their awareness of the purpose and function of monitoring.

In the final year of a course using self-directed learning, it is quite common for people to work in monitoring groups for up to two hours. These groups will have a steady membership and people will bring substantial pieces of work to be monitored. This work may well be included in the portfolio together with the comments made. It will provide evidence of counselling work as well as self and peer monitoring. Staff may well attend these groups, often offering a commentary on the work but also offering comments on the group process and acting as group consultants. They will ask:

- Has feedback been used?
- Are people monitoring themselves?
- Do they know what should be monitored?

Through having their work monitored by others, students will internalize questions which help them become more adept at self-monitoring. The hope and intention is that this becomes a lifetime habit – self-directing learners becoming self-monitoring practitioners.

Models

As students begin to ask what it is they should be monitoring and are shown how to monitor their skills they can be introduced to different models and also be given a method of skills analysis which allows specific behaviours to be identified and practised.

Micro skills

A useful example of skills analysis is to be found in Evison and Ronaldson's model of micro skills (Evison and Ronaldson, 1975). The approach focuses on some basic skills and gives students a vocabulary to describe what is happening between two people or in a group of people. It helps them be more conscious and more analytical regarding what they are doing. The focus is on the behaviour, not on the intention behind the behaviour. The skills are:

- seeking information
- reflecting feelings
- testing interpretations
- encouraging continuity
- agreeing
- disagreeing
- expressing feelings
- giving evaluation
- giving information
- prescribing
- giving interpretation.

The students will need training and practice in learning to distinguish and monitor these micro skills. To this end they can video themselves and analyse their use of these skills, and/or they can monitor existing video-tapes of, for example, Rogers, Perls or Ellis, members of staff or each other and ask themselves which skills each practitioner uses most frequently. Since students work as clients as well as counsellors, in the former role they are in an excellent position to give good feedback on the effect of the skills used. This helps the person in the role of counsellor to think about and monitor her use of various skills.

After a number of practice sessions students will be able to distinguish between the different skills and perhaps be coming up with others. Being able to name a skill helps students to become clearer about what they are doing. They may not feel that they are outstanding counsellors but will have received evidence that they can, for example, listen empathically, reflect and express feelings, confront effectively, focus a client on what is concerning her. They can be realistically confident of what they hope to offer their clients.

Interventions

John Heron's Six-Category Intervention Analysis (Heron, 1986), can also be used as a framework to identify interventions. There are six general categories of skills, and these can be further analysed into specific categories, using a micro skills approach. It is a very useful way of discriminating between different kinds of interventions. As students learn to analyse their interventions using these categories they become more aware of their accustomed ways of intervening and have the opportunity to alter them:

Prescriptive – giving personal opinions or advice
Informative – dealing with facts or information
Confrontative – giving challenge or direct feedback
Cathartic – releasing tension, helping to feel
Catalytic – responding and reflecting, clarifying, helping to think
Supportive – validating, offering encouragement, allowing.

The first three are designed to be mainly authoritative and the second three to be mainly facilitative. They are value-neutral and no one particular category is more important than another; their importance depends on their appropriate use within a context. They must be used supportively. Within each intervention category the micro skills listed earlier can be identified. The students can be encouraged to monitor the effect of the intervention within a workshop, with a client, and in the large group. They can be encouraged to notice if, for example, an intervention that was intended to be cathartic enabled the expression of feeling and, if not, why not. What could have been done differently?

These models can be taught, practised and offered to students as a useful starting point. They can work with them on the course and in their professional settings. They may wish to adapt them, change them, ignore them or learn more about them, but integrating the skills from these models offers a concrete way of adopting a facilitative approach with others and of analysing habitual ways of communicating.

The models will support self-directed learning if they are offered at the point when students recognize the need for them. As they attempt to monitor their work students realize they need an analytical tool. They want to be able to select interventions that will fulfil a particular purpose: for example, enable a client to experience her feelings more profoundly.

Uses of monitoring

Monitoring can be used to support learning. Ideas are passed on. For example, people may be inspired by watching others to use art forms to express understanding or to offer to the client a way of communicating other than with words. Students can learn about the use of metaphor and drama in counselling and discover that there are models they do not yet know much about. This mode of learning provides students with the option of asking for or organizing workshops on these topics. Through their practice, they are gaining concrete information about what skills or knowledge would help them both as people and to become more effective as practitioners; this gives them ideas for other workshops that they will want to ask for or organize.

Above all, through monitoring her own work and that of others, the student can make the link between theory and practice. During a monitoring exercise it is possible to notice whether or not people are picking up the culture of self-direction or whether they are still looking for external direction. As they counsel their 'client' they will be encouraging that 'client' to find and follow a direction that is right for her.

Some students enjoy monitoring their work in private: they may make a tape recording or a very detailed process recording and monitor their work on their own. Later this work may be shown to a supervisor or added to the portfolio.

Problems

Self and peer monitoring is not easy. There are many blocks to effective monitoring. On a self-directed course it is possible students may say that it is not what they need to do or learn about. This may be a genuine objection, and may also cover a fear of being seen or observed at work. Possibly there is a great deal of 'baggage' dating back to exposing their weaknesses at school and receiving extremely negative messages about themselves if they did not 'get it right'. In such a situation staff would work extremely hard to meet the students' fear and distress and help them find ways of handling it. They might offer counselling, support, or set up monitoring opportunities that felt as safe as possible, and, above all, ask the student what she needs in order to do this task well. The relevance of self and peer monitoring to the original contract on self and peer assessment should be pointed out.

After a certain amount of feedback and monitoring, there is likely to be some pressure from students to find out whether the work being done is good enough to help clients. Is it as good as or better than the work done on other courses? What else do students want to learn or practise in order to work well with others? What values underline the skills used?

EVALUATION

Evaluation, unlike monitoring and feedback, involves putting a value on a piece of work, saying whether or not it reaches a reasonable standard and whether or not the learning objectives set out at an early stage in the course have been reached. Students should be encouraged to set learning objectives with evaluation in mind. They consider what actions they will require of themselves in order to achieve their objectives, and what tangible evidence there will be to demonstrate that those objectives have been achieved. An evaluation of counselling practice should be in line with the overall philosophy. People should experience themselves as being in control of the methods of evaluation used. Evaluation should first of all be carried out by the student herself, since a self-directed form of learning aims to produce practitioners who can self-evaluate and who will continue to do so.

The staff will want the students to be vigilant in noticing how they are working and whether or not this is in line with their learning plan and with what they themselves set out to achieve. They will want the students to notice what value they place on the skills and knowledge they have gained. Self-evaluation builds on the feedback and self and peer monitoring that is in place and starts to give value to different interventions. The staff encourage and enhance the students' ability to self-evaluate by making sure they have had some models of good practice, that they have seen different models of counselling in operation and have had a chance to discuss these and hear the clients' views. Each student's client experience, both in exercises on the course and with her counsellor, helps to provide her with yardsticks. In some cases a student may decide to delay submitting her work for assessment or even decide that she is not on the right course of training. The hope generally is that students have gained enough self-awareness and self-knowledge from their experiences on the course to be able to make such decisions confidently and in their own self-interest.

The ability to evaluate is further enhanced when, after a workshop, the group gets together to discuss what went on and what 'worked'. This provides an opportunity for the students to evaluate each other's performance and to be explicit about important values within counselling. If evaluation starts early enough and is done frequently enough it will be possible to be quite clear about work that does not reach the required standard. Clear expectations and criteria can then be formed regarding what practice is acceptable.

It is useful to have a check-list of skills and ascertain which were used where and how well. Did an attempt to confront a client result in a useful change for that client? Did a cathartic intervention help the client experience more deeply? How do we know? Many things may have occurred and some of the most useful of these may not have been intended. In a group which is working well with a high degree of trust and honest feedback, it is possible to explore some of the unexpected and deeper levels of change that may be brought about. Although the counsellor may be making interventions aimed at a particular outcome, for example, helping the client to think through a problem, the client may gain a great deal more from the personality and behaviour of the counsellor and their developing relationship than from the particular skills used.

The student who has played the part of client and brought genuine client material is in a position to give extremely useful feedback and evaluation. She may have gained insight about past or present actions or states of mind, or ideas for future action. This may have been brought about through the powerful experience of receiving attention and being prepared to give that to herself, or through an effective direct verbal intervention from the counsellor. The client may have experienced a profound moment of communication which perhaps only she can evaluate. Talking about this can help the counsellor and the others to realize the limitations of focusing an evaluation procedure *only* on the successful application of skills. They will recognize that there has also been a degree of powerful communication that is difficult to quantify or measure. It will become clear to the students that counselling consists of something more than an accomplished performance of a number of skills. They are in a position to feel and understand the importance of the relationship between counsellor and client as an agent of change.

It is relatively easy for the students to evaluate the use of skills, but more difficult to place a value on the relationship. How do students gauge whether or not the 'client' felt held, safe, encouraged, challenged and supported? Was the 'client' able to communicate important thoughts and feelings and have them taken further? These questions underline the importance of using authentic personal material in counsellor training, rather than role play.

It is by keeping in touch with themselves as clients as well as staying close to the standards of ethics and practice laid down by the British Association for Counselling, and by drawing on the experience and expertise of the staff, that students can place a value on the work they are doing, evolve standards and principles that are right for them as well as staying in touch with the values of their profession and peer group. When the students are evaluating out of their personal experience of being a client in a real way, albeit in a short training exercise, they are having a strong and important effect on standards. The method of evaluation being used is congruent with the principles of self-direction. The students are not being evaluated by an unknown external authority. They are staying in touch with their values about counselling and with what has been useful or otherwise to them as clients, and are able to use an internal locus of evaluation rather than accept imposed judgements.

Students will want to stay with this internal locus of evaluation when they move to self and peer assessment. They will want to create a method of assessment that is not oppressive of individuals but is respectful of their rights and also safeguards standards of practice. It will be necessary to decide if a good enough standard has been reached and what kind of assessment is philosophically compatible with self-directed learning.

SELF AND PEER ASSESSMENT

The final assessment on a course is concerned with deciding whether or not the desired standard has been reached. The awarding of a qualification is at stake; and the assessors decide in the light of evaluation whether or not their fellow students' work reaches an acceptable standard.

Assessment is a highly political activity. If the students do not feel that they have a major part in deciding on assessment they will not be genuinely free to direct themselves in their learning. They will be influenced by what they believe will be required of them in the final assessment and by their perception and fears about other people's criteria. There is nothing to be gained by letting a student work on through a course only to find at the end that she has not met a standard imposed by others and measured by criteria that she took no part in forming or agreeing.

In order to prepare for a final assessment it is useful if students have taken part in previous assessments (sometimes called formative or mock assessments), which give them practice at assessing and being assessed and also a better idea of what standards they have reached.

The concept of self and peer assessment is congruent with a course that aims to reflect and parallel a person-centred approach to education. This was the method used on the South West London and Southwark Colleges counselling courses. It is made clear to the students during the preparatory and introductory stages (see Chapter 4) that they will be expected to take responsibility for their own and other people's assessment and that they will devise structures for doing this.

In the early days of the South West London College course no staff assessment of any kind was offered. In later years the staff asked for a piece of self assessed work from each student and in the first two years of the course assessed the self assessment, which meant that they were making some contribution to a formative assessment. The form of the final assessment was still left to the students to decide upon and administer.

Students are encouraged during the course to form a clear opinion of what a skilled practitioner of counselling skills should be able to do when she has completed a course of counsellor training. Assessment involves deciding whether or not students are capable of doing this, and a group of self-directing learners must come up with a way of making that decision.

It could be argued that self assessment is the only form that is compatible with self-directed learning. If the individual is responsible for directing her learning, perhaps only she can assess it. The ability of the individual to assess herself is a mark of her maturity and ability to practise. She has enough experience now to know the difference between bad and good counselling, from the perspectives of a client, a counsellor and a trained observer. She has also learned to recognize good and bad practice in others and to find ways of passing on her opinions, views and decisions.

Taking responsibility for learning means taking responsibility for assessing that learning. A truly independent learner will be organizing her own criteria for assessment and will assess herself. Staff will encourage students to do this and discuss these self assessments with their supervisors. The supervisor's comments are there as a safeguard against bad practice and also as part of a formative assessment that might challenge the student to go further in her learning. Tutors give comprehensive tutorials when the work required each year is handed in and the self assessments discussed. Their aim is to develop each student's skill at self assessment.

Although self assessment is vital for all counsellors, it is not sufficient for the awarding of a qualification that must stand up to comparison with others that use a more conventional method of assessment. In addition, self-directing students learn within a community and in an organization for learning that they have helped create. Other students have been involved in their learning, and those students have an interest in a just and fair assessment. Moreover, self-monitoring and self-evaluating professionals will wish to be accountable to others for their work and its assessment. They will want that work witnessed, acknowledged and measured by common criteria, for they know that sometimes their judgements may be biased and, for the sake of clients, will want them ratified.

The counselling courses at South West London and Southwark Colleges used self and peer assessment. This was the agreement that the students entered into when they started the course, and the system offers encouragement to all to take joint responsibility for the standards reached and offered to clients. Each year created its own system, helped to a greater or lesser degree by the work of previous students. Staff and students often spent extended periods of time in large groups hammering out the right criteria and an appropriate method by which to self and peer assess. Despite numerous disagreements over a number of issues it was always clear to each year group that all students should be answerable to the same criteria and use the same assessment structure. The staff shared this view; it was never acceptable for an individual or for groups to devise separate criteria or methods of assessment. A great deal of hard work and thought contributed to creating a good system of self and peer assessment.

The first step was to create a Community Contract. This is a development of the ground rules which were arrived at in the early stages of the life of the learning group. It sets out the values of the group of learners, what it sees as good counselling and how it intends to assess the evidence of counselling skills. This contract or working agreement is discussed further in Chapter 3.

In deciding on an assessment procedure, students should consider issues such as who they want to be assessed by, who they would like to assess and what this says about the way they want their own assessment to be carried out. By picking out people whose assessment they would respect they are of course doing some overt assessment themselves. People need to think about themselves in the role of assessor. They should consider what groups of people they would have difficulty assessing or would like to assess. What constitutes a good assessment? What tendencies towards rescuing or persecuting are likely to be evoked by assessment? Again, after many hours of discussion and argument a procedure is arrived at, sometimes in the large group itself, sometimes by a small group being given a mandate to go away and finalize a suitable method.

One method that was devised by the students gave each student two random assessors and allowed them to choose a third. Assessors then took the student's portfolio away to read and decided whether or not it met the requirements of the Community Contract and the student's personal learning contract and self assessment. They were expected to assess the portfolio and not the student! On assessment day the assessors met with their assessees to give feedback on the work and in most cases to give the final result. Sometimes assessment groups asked for a facilitator, possibly a staff member, to be with them to help them look at the way they worked. The group attempted to reach a consensus regarding pass, fail or refer. Where it did not reach a consensus or there was an appeal, new assessors were appointed and the assessment went ahead as before. (The possibility of mutual assessment or further appeals was discussed at the planning stage and ruled out: the former was thought to be inequitable and the second impossible within the time restrictions of the course.) There were often flaws in the procedures and very difficult situations arose where people who worked together found themselves assessing each other. No foolproof solutions were ever arrived at and it had to be conceded that self and peer assessment systems, like other methods, were fraught with difficulties.

Both staff and students may find the staff role an ambiguous one when it comes to assessment. Staff may start to feel guilty that they have declined traditional staff responsibility and perhaps are asking too much from the students. They encourage the students to use them as consultants and for academic and personal support. The students need the support and expertise of the staff to reassure themselves that although the system they have devised is far from perfect it is good enough. The staff in turn need the same reassurance from the external assessors. The students can feel quite reticent and fearful with each other and angry with the staff. As the staff are not assessing it can seem safe to pass all anger and resentment on to them rather than for two people who might be assessing each other to work out their difficulties and try to reach some resolution. Part of the reason for the constant encouragement of straightforward communication and effective feedback in the early stages of the course is so that people can become accustomed to addressing difficulties with each other as near as possible to the time they occur and do not leave resentments to prejudice the final assessment.

Workshops on assessment help people to face up to their role within the system of peer assessment. The developmental aspect of peer assessment becomes evident as people consider themselves in the role of assessor and realize that they are responsible for their own assessment and that of others. Assessment becomes something they must be concerned with for the sake of their professional standards and the welfare of clients.

Students also struggle to come to terms with the role of the external assessors, whose task is not to decide who should become a counsellor, but to assess the assessment procedure and the course itself. They are also there as moderators to ensure that the standards reached are comparable with those on other courses. They can be transformed into hostile, threatening figures and can appear to have a great deal more power than, in this particular system, they have been given. It is as though the students cannot believe that they are responsible for the final assessment. Understandably, they hope that perhaps, in the last analysis, someone else will take this on.

Ideally, in a healthy group there will be a considerable amount of participation in assessment. People will have come to realize that the counselling course is something that they have helped to create, and have directed their learning in specific ways which are useful to them. They may well have changed radically since the start of the course, and they want that learning and those changes to be recognized. Therefore, it matters deeply to them that they are assessed in a way that will measure their unique learning and personal change. Of course, the non-ideal will happen. People may become apathetic or bored by protracted discussions in the large group. A dominant group of students may take command and organize the assessment procedure. These issues of ownership and control are of major significance in counselling (see Chapter 3). They are highlighted during assessment as people become clear about how they do or do not exercise control, and how power is taken or given away. In particular, they notice for themselves whether they have acted as they would have done in the past or whether they have taken advantage of a very dynamic challenge to be involved co-operatively in the creation of a new system.

People can develop with the help of good formative assessments which are carried out all the way through the course and built on in the final assessment. In the early phase of a course of training staff organize an extensive community workshop on self and peer assessment. This can be set up as follows:

Students work in pairs and then in small groups to decide on their key criteria for self assessment. These are written up and made available for the whole group to see and discuss. It is suggested that people use some of these criteria to assess their work and include the results in their portfolio, or use the results to start their portfolio. In order to make a gentle start on the task of peer assessment the students each choose two or three people to give them some feedback on the way they worked in groups on the course. They are reminded about how to give feedback effectively. Strong feelings may be raised by the exercise and a generous amount of group processing time may be necessary at the end to draw out the issues and principles raised and allow people to resolve and integrate their feelings.

Staff organize the first workshop of this nature. Later, students can be encouraged to organize workshops for themselves and to welcome a culture of frequent formative assessments.

As staff witness the final stage of self and peer assessment they may well begin to wonder whether in fact they are depriving the students by not offering a staff view of their work. The staff's experience and skill would certainly enable them to give an informed judgement about students' work, and without this the students may be deprived of an important element in their training. It remains all the more necessary that the staff give their contributions in the formative processes described in this chapter and devote a considerable amount of energy and skill to training the students to evaluate and assess their counselling work themselves.

The tasks of assessment highlight issues of power and control among the students. They have authority and are challenged to use it with integrity. For many it is one of the greatest challenges of their lives. They must acknowledge what they deem to be good practice and judge others in the light of clear criteria based on this. They must create and carry out a method of self and peer assessment which validates their belief that people can direct and manage their own learning.

Throughout the course students should be recording and demonstrating their learning. This results in the production of a portfolio, which forms an essential part of the assessment procedure. It generally provides a learning record, a personal journal and evidence of counselling skills and knowledge.

THE PORTFOLIO

One of the built-in requirements of self-directed learning is that students make their work available to others. Normally they produce a portfolio of work which demonstrates their use of counselling and/or counselling skills. Decisions regarding the contents, length and form of the portfolio are devolved to the students. They are asked to set common criteria for assessment of the portfolio and to decide what should be in it in order to provide material for effective assessment.

Ideally the portfolio should be started in the first year. It can be used as a diary of development for the student to record her progress. Through this written record she is able to ensure that her experience is available to others, both for their learning and in order to make herself accountable within the group of self-managing learners.

Peer assessment of the portfolio sharpens this process considerably and emphasizes the responsibility that learners have towards one another. Students find that thinking of themselves carrying out the role of assessor helps them present their work in an assessable and accessible form.

Most portfolios contain a section entitled something like 'My journey to the course'. This describes past achievements and personal history. It also allows people to become aware of, and to announce, the skills and knowledge they already have. They are encouraged to understand and describe their strengths and this gives them confidence to describe their continuing learning needs. Through the portfolio the student's previous life and work can be accredited.

Writing the portfolio is in itself a process of personal development. Several years after leaving a course that used a model of self-directed learning, a student wrote:

> The hardest thing to do was to begin! And the way I began was to spend a whole day trying to create an interwoven diagram of my experience and learning over the three years and the development and the inter-relationship between that and my personal work and counselling self. It was important for me to have an over-view of my time and the inter-connections (network of relationships) before I could try and separate out the different parts to be written about.

The portfolio will typically contain a copy of the student's personal contract, her learning plan, the Community Contract, her philosophy of counselling, different examples of the use of counselling or counselling skills in her work, a description of her preferred theoretical model, an account of her use of supervision, written feedback from peers, evidence that she has become a reflective self-monitoring practitioner, and written evidence of self and peer assessment. She will have shown how she is able to consider and learn from personal experience and how she intends to change and develop. Her authorship and ownership of the portfolio symbolizes the fact that she has taken care of her own learning.

The brief for the portfolio is a wide one. There is generally strong encouragement for students to describe the skills and experience that they have brought to the course. The skills used in bringing up children and housekeeping are seen as relevant and important. Portfolio-based learning encourages the use of a wide range of experience and skills. The portfolio may not be written but may be a taped presentation or may make use of approaches such as art therapy, visualization, poetry or other media. People are encouraged to communicate in a number of different ways and the less verbal are afforded an opportunity to communicate in a way they are comfortable with. The portfolio also offers an opportunity to be very creative. A complex tapestry of skills, knowledge, subjective experience and personal history is offered for peer assessment.

The portfolio allows individuals to give others access to the skills and knowledge they use within their work setting. They find that their skills are acknowledged and that others would like to acquire them. The students learn a great deal about other people's professional practice.

They use the challenge of portfolio writing to think about and become clearer regarding the theoretical model they find of most use to them. Again through reading other people's portfolios they have access to other models and can see how these are being put into practice.

Above all, the portfolio is a place where the learner's philosophy of counselling is developed and made known. She can also demonstrate the personal relevance of the learning experiences of the last three years.

WORKSHOPS

A workshop consists of a group of people coming together to share experience and knowledge and develop skills. It is within workshops that students learn about different models of counselling and become aware of some of the relevant themes and topics. Workshops provide an opportunity to acquire skills and knowledge from the staff and other students. They generally provide an opportunity to practise observation and feedback.

The emphasis in workshops is on experiential learning. The staff member does not present herself as an expert on the theme of the workshop and does not aim to pour knowledge into empty minds. She aims to provide opportunities and facilitate their use. She encourages the students to take responsibility for the learning process by becoming very clear about what they want to learn from a series of workshops on a particular topic and how they want to learn those things. They help plan the curriculum, making sure that it is in line with their learning plan, and they evaluate the results. The use of their personal experience as a vehicle for their own and others' learning ensures that they are highly involved in the content and method.

Students will choose workshops which will support a particular speciality. For instance, someone who wishes to work using Gestalt will do her best to ensure that workshops using this method will appear on the timetable; individual members of staff will have their individual styles within workshops, but generally students will be encouraged to state clearly what it is they want and need to learn about Gestalt and how they see themselves applying that to their work.

It is the students who plan the year's timetable. In some cases workshops are run by students. Staff insist that there is at least one module of counselling skills on the timetable in the foundation year and that each year group engages in a process of self and peer assessment towards the end of the year. In the counselling skills workshops the skills of giving effective feedback and of monitoring each other's work are introduced by the staff who run them. Consideration is also given to the BAC code of ethics.

Other workshop topics could be sexuality, working with child sexual abuse, art therapy, psychosynthesis, person-centred counselling, psycho-analysis. There are probably as many styles and kinds of workshop as there are staff and students. A model for a workshop that combines evaluation, teaching, feedback, a chance to look at the culture and context of coun-selling as well as simply giving time for practice and the opportunity for performance could be as follows:

EXAMPLE

Small groups consisting of at least four people are formed, and the following roles taken:

counsellor
client
observer(s)
reflective enquirer(s)

Counsellor and client work together for an agreed length of time on a matter that is of some concern for the client.

The observer feeds back what she sees, hears and perceives. This could cover a number of points that have been agreed in advance and may include descrip-tion of behaviour, such as body language, eye movements, gestures and physical stance and how these change, diminish or increase as the session continues. The observer might notice at what points the counsellor leans forward or backward and what the client is saying or doing at this time. Is there an observable reac-tion in the client?

There is also some commentary on the use of questions, interpretations, reflection of feeling and reflection of content. The observer(s) may wish to make use of the micro skill description mentioned above or may have an alternative list of skills that the counsellor has asked them to notice.

The reflective enquirer comes in at another level, asking questions designed to elicit how the counsellor is thinking about her work, what goals and how she sets these.

She may also be interested in the cultural implications of the interaction in this setting at this time. There is an opportunity to think about the basis from which she counsels, the antecedents of the counselling model or models being used. She may also wish to use John Heron's analysis (Heron, 1986) or some other model that would increase awareness of the possible elements or intentions involved in any communication and whether or not the intervention succeeds.

The staff member works with the group, either as a teacher and/or demon-strator of counselling skills or in a more supervisorial or consultative capacity. She will ask people to move between the roles, noticing as they do so what has been or can be learned from each role. She will make sure that the client is asked for her thoughts and reactions and that both client and counsellor are given a chance to de-role. After such a session the student playing the counsellor's role will have a much clearer idea of what further skills she needs and of the values placed on the ones she has. She will be encouraged to self-evaluate and self assess.

There is a sense in which a counsellor should always be in touch with all of the four roles as she works. Certainly she needs to become a reflective enquirer into the process that goes on between herself and her client. Work in a self-directing community encourages people to reflect constantly on the way they are managing their relationships. The counsellor does this with the client and also helps her become reflective about herself. The counsellor should remember how it feels to be a client and use that knowledge for the client's benefit.

The group may also wish to draw attention to the way the counsellor elicits feeling, what choices she makes, what her particular method of, for example, making a reflection is. What skills does she use in order to be cathartic or supportive? Participants in such an exercise are becoming skilled perceivers and thoughtful critics through comparing the different ways of conducting a counselling session. It is through the skilled participation and subtle facilitation of the staff member or student facilitator that workshops such as the one just described supply the machinery for learning.

Students who choose to learn about counselling in this self-managing way take more responsibility for their learning than do members of a more conventional course. It is important that they do this from a celebratory standpoint. Staff members and other students should interrupt any tendencies towards being overly critical or self-denigratory. The student can be encouraged to celebrate the joy and fascinating potential of being human. She directs her learning above all to continue to develop and increase the possibilities for being creative. She appreciates and accepts herself. She does this with others and encourages them to do the same.

As the students work to create a democratic relationship which will enable people to feel free to learn, many of the issues which haunt democracies make themselves visible and will need addressing. Staff and students will want to know how to make democratic relationships work in this particular environment. Power, staff/student relationships, creating safety, bias and prejudice are just some of the important concerns in a self-directed learning community. They are challenging, exciting and highly relevant to counselling. The looser structure and greater freedom to choose afford a space where interpersonal and group processes are very clearly highlighted. The next chapter considers how staff and students can work together to clear some of the obstacles to self-directed learning.

THREE
Issues in self-directed learning

Self-directed learning offers many challenges to trainers and students, challenges which highlight important issues of personal and political power within the counselling process itself. These can be very clearly addressed in the forum of a self-directed course, in which students aim to create a community which is self-governing and self-regulating.

This chapter discusses the role of the staff in helping people to be self-directing; the use and abuse of power; the political nature of counselling; and the importance of culture and history as an element of any empathic relationship.

THE ROLE OF STAFF

The staff must be good counsellors. They must listen and reflect. They must be sensitive to interpersonal and group processes. They must use the strengths within the group and encourage co-operation so that useful working agreements – those which encourage learning – are made. They must safeguard and strengthen those agreements and contracts. Their interventions must convey the belief that students are responsible for their own learning.

Staff on self-directed learning courses have relinquished traditional roles and have invited the students into a power-sharing relationship with them. Each new group of students works out how to handle this and experiments with independence, counterdependence and interdependence in the way they relate to individual members of staff and to the staff as a group. They come to regard the staff as people with expertise who can be worked with as peers and consultants. The fact that the staff are not the ultimate assessors of the students' work allows for a relationship between peers.

The staff challenge traditional concepts of leadership. They ask people to notice for themselves what kinds of help they need and to ask for that help. They encourage the students to exercise leadership skills. Students are helped to find out what they want to learn and how they want to learn it and are facilitated in doing so. The staff's task in the early stages is of group facilitation and group management. Later they will also have a more conventional training role, sharing their expertise as experienced practitioners within workshops where skills are taught and demonstrated.

The staff take a proactive role in helping students learn. They are particularly visible at the start of a course but would expect, by the end, to move towards a mainly supportive position.

The staff will offer a relationship where the student feels accepted and in which she begins to accept herself, possibly for the first time. This is an essential experience, and one that the trainee counsellor will later offer to her clients. In this relationship the student can begin to let go of the old self concept, the false self which was formed in response to a desire to please others. Having learned to accept herself, she will become more accepting of others.

The staff are generally counsellors or therapists themselves. They espouse a belief in an individual's capacity for change and in her essential goodness. They work from a belief in human potential rather than to remedy a deficiency or fill a space or lack.

Students are encouraged to trust the authority within themselves. While staff may choose to act authoritatively from time to time, they are essentially aiming to work as peers with their students. They focus on helping people develop their own resources rather than on supplying knowledge or skills which they as staff judge to be useful.

The staff must direct their own learning so that they understand the difficulties which face students when they direct themselves. It is in the way they are, rather than in what they say, that the staff communicate about being self-directing. The role is less central, although no less important, than that of the traditional teacher or trainer. Indeed, they are occupied with bringing about a more intense change: a change in consciousness within an individual or group. This will involve role stress and challenge for themselves and they should ensure that they have access to suitable support systems.

Staff should be clear about their role and the power they have in situations where the student feels vulnerable. Students will sometimes think that all previous learning has been useless and that they have nothing to fall back on. They are then likely to become extremely dependent as they take the necessary steps to move from conscious incompetence to conscious competence. It is of primary importance that staff offer an accepting relationship where there is support for the students as they practise new skills and competencies. Students will be challenged in this approach to learning and may need to be helped to find counselling and support from sources within and outside the course. Without appropriate help at crucial stages in their progress students may doubt themselves and their ability to move forward. It is the staff member's task to help people decide what kind of help would be useful to them and to offer guidance in obtaining it.

Staff are the recipients of projections in this model of learning, as in any other. They will be called upon to respond to these and to be aware of their own projections. Ideally, they will talk about these experiences to the students and examine their significance. This should enable the student to work with her clients' projections. Staff will notice how projections and other defence mechanisms impinge on the life of the large or small groups. They encourage the students to notice this for themselves, to learn constantly from what is happening in the present.

While the staff member does not determine goals or provide all the resources, she is not simply an ordinary member of the group: her greater experience has taught her to be receptive to all the learning opportunities that arise. A number of other tasks follow on from this: becoming aware of how resources are being used, how people are relating to each other, who speaks most and to whom, how power is being distributed, and whether or not the dynamics operating in more formal organizations are being applied in this setting. For example: are highly articulate people more powerful in this setting? If so, can this be redressed or offset?

It may well be that in the early stages of the course the staff are more aware of the way the group is operating than the students. However, it will be expected that the students will soon take this role as well. An ability to work effectively in groups is part of the armoury of skills that the student will be encouraged to acquire by the time she finishes her course. In all of this the trainer is very much part of the group. She does not withdraw from the learner but learns alongside her and models the stance of taking as much self-responsibility as possible. She wants the student to become conscious of her power and responsibility in learning and hopes to bring about this change in consciousness by being powerful and responsible herself. Once she makes interventions she becomes present, releasing energy, becoming a role model, a force to be reckoned with, someone to be admired, and challenged. She communicates self-acceptance and conveys a sense of safety about self-revelation.

Staff need to challenge students. As most teachers know, there is a moment to give a student a good push. Some students will consciously seek it. Others will avoid it ferociously and perhaps must be left to do so; their avoidance can be commented on and they may be asked what they need to do in order to move on and take risks. Comments and challenges should be offered in the light of the core conditions that enhance counselling and personal growth. Staff challenge the students to notice how they are managing their learning, whether or not they are meeting their learning goals, how they are stopping themselves learning, what further help they need and how they will go about getting it.

The trainer is there as a role model and to provide a good safe and stimulating environment for learning. She does this by focusing on each opportunity for learning as it arises; by making useful, well-timed interventions; by providing structure when she judges that to be necessary; and by not providing structure when she judges that it would be more helpful for others to learn about providing it. For example, if students choose to conduct a group themselves, the staff member will offer support in the planning, execution and evaluation. She will also comment on her own work as a staff member and welcome feedback on that.

Finally, the staff member needs to rely on her influence and expertise to meet her own needs as a facilitator of learning and as a practitioner of self-direction. The ambiguity of the role provides stress: the staff member cannot hide behind being an expert. She is working with mature people who have their own distinct area of expertise. By encouraging the students to follow their inner authority and direction she is likely to find herself continuously challenged. On the other hand, she is needed as a refuge when students feel insecure, and students' anxieties may well, at times, provoke similar feelings in her. Unlike the conventional trainer she does not have control, and this too gives rise to anxiety. She should also become redundant as the students become more autonomous, and this can evoke strong feelings of uselessness and futility. She must be able to handle this and resist encouraging the students to become dependent on her. Far from taking up a detached position, she is very much a member of the group, feeling and thinking with them and with her own personal and learning agenda.

STAFF SELF-MANAGEMENT

The staff must be able to manage themselves as individuals and as a group and to be role models in this for the students. They should become as aware as possible of any rivalry or tensions so that these can be worked with in a professional manner and not impede their work with students. They may struggle with the difficulties of doing this within a hierarchical structure. Other staff within the same educational institution will be working in a more traditional way and will not understand the support and development requirements of colleagues using self-directed learning. The counselling staff decide how to manage themselves as a group and create their own models and ways of doing this.

If staff are committed to a self-directed way of working, this will be reflected in the way they work together and in the management structure they devise for themselves. They require an agreement regarding self and peer monitoring and a way of dividing and allocating tasks. They should have time for sessions devoted to developing and thinking about their courses and their interpretation of self-direction. They will want to think of innovative ways of supporting the students' freedom and autonomy in learning. These sessions will have to be organized, facilitated and paid for.

Staff will find it helpful to have a contract to support and challenge each other. Team teaching, peer supervision, regular meetings, development days and weekends and peer consultation with other courses are all ways for staff to examine and improve the quality of their work. Staff should arrange their own supervision in which to explore personal and professional concerns.

POWER AND AUTHORITY

The nature of power over others is a key issue in counselling and has to be considered in counsellor training. It is particularly relevant in a consideration of self-directedness. Students accept the idea that they are responsible for choosing their timetable but find it quite easy to 'forget' that they are responsible for their own assessment. The tendency is always to assume that someone else will tell them how good or bad their work is, whereas the staff would like to help students respect their own judgement of themselves and of their work and to be open to feedback and, ultimately to judgement from others. The question is always to know how much to 'feed' people and how much to stand back and let them experience their power and helplessness. Struggles for power are highlighted during planning times in the large group. The staff deliberately avoid taking control and consequently fights for power and influence among students are more intense than on a traditionally run course. This creates a power vacuum which is inevitably accompanied by envy, jealousy, competitiveness and a considerable amount of sibling rivalry as the students struggle to fill it. Constantly working out the difficulties involved in sharing power within a group of peers can raise awareness of the different ways individuals exert power and influence. Students have the opportunity to see the way individuals and groups attempt at both a conscious and an unconscious level to control others. Noticing this, working with it and still aiming to produce structures that enable learning by strengthening autonomy can be a preparation for creating and preserving a democratic relationship with a client.

Sometimes a small group of students will assume a leadership role. If this group remains constant, its members may act like and be treated as an alternative staff group. Staff and/or other students might deal with this by drawing attention to it and asking the whole group what they are doing with their power, whether they have found a way to direct themselves or whether they are a new self-appointed hierarchy. For the 'alternative staff' there may also be a dilemma in that they may be people who find it hard to tolerate a power vacuum and who find it difficult to bear their clients' chaotic struggles for personal autonomy. For them, support and strengthening is required to help them not to take power, while other students struggle and experiment with finding and acknowledging their ability to act powerfully.

Power struggles in a group are important because they bring interpersonal issues into the open to be dealt with in a transparent way. Learning to deal with power struggles in a supportive learning environment can provide a model for working with issues of power and control in the students' work settings and provide an opportunity for the different ways power is exercised interpersonally to be described, identified and examined, for example through the use of reward and punishment or giving or withholding expertise and information.

The question of power sharing, jealousy and envy can be addressed in the following ways:

1 *Group sculpts*, i.e. one or more people in a group place the other group members in positions which represent their psychological significance to the rest of the group.
2 *Power lines*, i.e. people form a line with the most powerful members at one end and the least powerful at the other. They can do this for themselves or be placed in a line by others. They can then experiment with moving and notice the feelings evoked.
3 *Workshops on envy and jealousy*.

Group sculpts

The group sculpts and the power lines are intended to help people move away from long discussions and intellectualizations about power and use exercises where the feelings are felt and highlighted. In a group sculpt one person, or a small group of people, is asked to arrange the others in order of their perceived significance in the group. This results in people being moved around like statues, with the most significant people being placed in the centre of the sculpt and others being moved out to the periphery. Such a workshop is invariably controversial and confronting for people have strong feelings about being perceived as powerful or powerless. A considerable amount of time needs to be set aside to work with the feelings that are aroused.

Power lines

In a power line the students arrange themselves in a hierarchical line in terms of how powerful or powerless they feel. They might experiment with moving to different positions in the line. They notice who they are standing next to and how they feel about that. They notice that by experimenting and placing themselves in different positions they are actually using their power. There is a great deal of experiential learning in such an exercise. It tends to be one of the experiences that is remembered most vividly and referred back to most frequently.

Workshops on envy and jealousy

The aim of these workshops is to break through the intellectual discussion and reach the feelings, the unique personal experience of people in the group.

One workshop which dealt with the difficult topic of envy and jealousy was run with the idea of looking at some of the held or hidden feelings in the student group. The idea of peer status is sometimes confused with the idea of equality. The students are *not* equal to each other or to the staff: there are differences in ethnic, educational, cultural, economic and religious background, and in personal attractiveness and inter-personal skills. Students may envy each other and experience jealousy over relationships with others. There is competition over attention and affection from the staff as well as from other students. These feelings can be hard to handle and difficult to talk about, and yet they are so significant to peer learning and assessment that ways of dealing with them should be sought.

In this particular workshop students were asked to work in co-counselling pairs, remembering and re-experiencing times in their lives when they felt envious or jealous. They then worked in a new pair, allowing themselves to become aware of whom in the room they felt envious or jealous of. People then wrote out 'envy' cards, and then milled around handing the cards to people of whom they were envious. This was confronting: some people received a lot of envy cards, some very few or none at all. People with several envy cards worked together on what it was like to be envied and the others worked on their feelings about not being envied. There was then a guided fantasy on jealousy and again people worked in small groups, processing the feelings that arose during that experience. The whole exercise, which lasted three hours, ended with discussion and feedback in the large group.

The large group itself also provides a forum in which constantly to address the exercise of power. Students frequently become both upset and angry at having to face their own power and powerlessness. Concerns about power, rivalry and anger should be noticed and acted upon as they arise so that the students feel reasonably clear about them when monitoring and assessing each other's work. The staff, who are likely to be struggling with similar feelings, will be much tested. They must be sufficiently clear of their own distress to be able to help and support the students.

It can be seen that vying for leadership, rivalry, envy, competition and conflict are inevitable as the students struggle to construct a timetable and a clear working agreement that will facilitate their learning. The staff are challenged to make this a useful experience. They do this in the ways just mentioned, and by establishing safe boundaries, by calling attention to what is happening, by encouraging people to relate this to their personal histories and by using the issues in the group to illuminate the dynamics in the relationship with a client. If power struggles are addressed clearly and openly, students will begin to feel safe enough to express real needs.

CREATING A SAFE ENVIRONMENT

The staff take a proactive role in creating a suitable climate for learning. They give a lead in the early stages by offering structures, exercises and other opportunities for people to work together. At the initial introductory weekend they devise exercises to enable students to be sure of their needs and expectations of the course. They may initiate the formation of temporary support groups or counselling triads or partnerships (see Chapter 4, p. 60). They do what they can to ensure that the course group offers a cohesive and supportive culture without creating a cosy niche away from the real world. They do this by encouraging the formation of a co-operative group with a permeable boundary. The group has a distinct identity but remains in contact with the rest of the college, and with other counselling courses and ways of working, welcoming guest lecturers and keeping in touch with the British Association for Counselling and other relevant bodies.

However, on a counselling course staff are ultimately responsible for the boundaries. They defend these against a great deal of testing and disagreement. Dissent is held and used creatively. The staff do not defend themselves against challenge and disagreement: they hear it, try to distinguish between the rational and irrational elements and see it in terms of the history of the group. They use it to teach about group dynamics.

On a self-directed course, which has unique norms and values, people are seeing themselves with new eyes. This means moving away from the harmonious self-concept which they have been building over the years to one which has many unexpected twists and turns. The move away from apparent harmony is challenging. Students may well be confronting a new self at a mature age and will want and need to know that life support mechanisms are available during this time of rebirth.

Through creative intervention and creative holding back, by ensuring secure boundaries, by drawing on their skills and knowledge as counsellors and therapists, staff create an infrastructure which enables people to clarify their expectations, form a learning group and establish a fruitful climate for learning.

INSTITUTIONAL SUPPORT

Within the host institution the course tutor or course director will be the person mainly concerned with interpreting and communicating about self-direction to others within the college or university. Staff using these ideas in conventional organizations will have problems: they will be introducing a model which contradicts the hierarchical structures that surround them. For some conventional managers, courses using self-directed learning are threatening and even dangerous. Such programmes challenge ideas about hierarchies. They threaten hard-won positions of seniority and power. Staff in charge of courses promulgating self-directed learning will usually be in precarious middle-management positions where they will be dealing with the stress of both junior and senior staff and need to communicate the ideas of both to each other. If the methods involved in self-directed learning are not fully understood within the college or university, members of staff will be questioned and possibly reprimanded for allowing some of the unstructured and seemingly chaotic exercises or events that take place in self-directed learning.

Ideas about peer assessment may not be looked on favourably by college authorities. Some traditional managers may wonder aloud why staff are being paid while students are seen running their own small groups, workshops or seminars. It can be difficult to convey the ideas implicit in self-directed learning.

Thus such courses are likely to be misunderstood within most traditional educational establishments. However, when college principals and others visit a self-directed course they are generally struck by the industrious atmosphere and have described workshops as magnetic. Visitors are generally less impressed by the idea of working in large groups to construct timetables or community contracts and may find it hard to accept self and peer assessment. The labour-intensive nature of counselling courses makes them vulnerable to attack, particularly in recent years when funds have been scarce. Most of the staff in other departments will teach in a more traditional way, although there are always some who are interested in and open to the ideas in self-directed learning. It can be very helpful and encouraging to work with the forces in favour rather than engage in defensive battles. There may be committees or working parties in the college to which counselling staff can make useful contributions. There are also likely to be other courses which would benefit from the skills and knowledge of people involved in counselling. Staff on other courses may well be able to contribute to the counselling course.

COMBATING RACISM, SEXISM, BIAS, ETC.

It is important to find ways of supporting the learning of *all* without diluting the philosophy of self-direction. This needs to be tackled in a multiplicity of ways which change and develop over time.

Staff convey the belief that by being in touch with their needs and wants students will enhance their opportunities to develop and learn. Students hear this expectation and begin to have it of themselves. Excited by the discovery that their learning can be related to their personal wants and needs, they should also be made aware that this is conditional on events in the real world. As self-directing learners they will be faced with obstacles and limitations. They can plan their learning in accordance with their needs but this does not guarantee that all their needs will be met.

Bias and prejudice are obstacles to the self-direction of the individual learner. If, in a large heterogeneous group of students, there is an unconscious tendency to downplay or ignore the contributions of, for example, black people, then it will be much more difficult for those black people to acknowledge their needs publicly and have assistance at getting them met. It is important for white counsellors to hear and see that they are being racist and work to combat the inevitable tendency of a predominantly white group to discriminate in all sorts of subtle ways against a black minority. For instance, it may be that the suggestions of white people are taken up and agreed to much more often than those of black people.

A way of combating prejudice is to notice it and comment on it, when it happens and to actively work against it. Heterosexism, for example, could be challenged by ensuring that an exercise involving role play includes examples of a gay or lesbian lifestyle. If the people experiencing the prejudice are left on their own to work against it they will have little energy and time left to meet their learning goals. By combating prejudice the staff support the possibilities for self-direction among people who are often deprived of good opportunities for learning and the possibilities of directing their lives.

Clarity about the white European bias within counselling helps create empathy between black and white students. First-hand knowledge of the complexities arising when people of different race, sexual orientation or physical ability counsel each other is a significant attribute in a counselling trainer or trainee. This knowledge can be extended within the group of staff and students if people openly acknowledge and work with the examples of prejudice and bias that occur.

For example, in attempting to combat sexism it is important to be aware that social forces will support male power in many groups. Sometimes women in a group need to be supported in order to redress this. It may require a member of staff to facilitate this and for the staff as well as the students to have made a contract with each other to acknowledge the relevance of these dynamics and to heighten awareness about prejudice.

Sexual prejudice can sometimes operate in another way on counselling courses. Men are usually in a minority and can sometimes find themselves the butt of long-stored anger from women. Yet most men on counselling courses are, in intention at least, non-sexist and non-oppressive. It is a matter for concern when they find themselves representing all men, or the many men who are oppressive towards women. Men in such situations may feel themselves to be the objects of oppression: the same persecutory dynamics are being enacted. The challenge for a particular woman is to understand that she may be seeing men on the course as embodiments of men who have been abusive to her in the past. Or she may also be projecting her own aggressive tendencies onto male students. The task for the male student is to be aware of the restimulation caused by his presence and be prepared to examine ways in which he may be being oppressive. Staff will help students deal with these issues and work constantly to reown positive and negative projections.

Staff on self-directed learning courses have the task of encouraging this aspect of personal development as well as supporting equal opportunities as expressed in the college policies. Sometimes this can appear to be an impossible combination!

While these challenging situations provide unique opportunities to learn about the way oppression works in groups, it is important for staff to remember that students from minority groups are there primarily for their own learning, not in order to act as a challenge to others. Other students may need additional training, away from the course, in, for example, anti-racism.

Staff and students should continually be searching for ways in which equal opportunities can be increased. The main ways in which staff do this is by helping the students be clear about their personal and learning needs and encouraging them to continually monitor whether or not these are being met. Staff constantly try to make sure that students are not being ignored or excluded. They do this in formal ways through tutorials and through being informally available and accessible to individuals.

The course will benefit if the skills, resources, life histories and aspects of the culture of all its members are included. People from many different groups can be encouraged to make the course their own and learn from what is on offer. It is clear that learning opportunities for people whose racial or cultural origin, sexual orientation or physical abilities are different from the majority may be limited by that difference. The staff should devise ways of assessing the needs of these students and encouraging them to make it clear what particular help they need. Moreover, the staff on a counselling course should be looking towards the work with clients, many of whom will benefit enormously from their contact with counsellors who are not out of the standard mould.

Over time staff and students will find concrete ways to offset inequalities, e.g. providing materials in Braille for blind students, using visual aids which depict a multi-cultural community, including requests for lifts, ramps and ground floor rooms in their requests for new premises, offering more comprehensive booklists and learning aids and becoming slowly and painfully aware of the pervasive presumption of a white, heterosexual, able-bodied norm in counselling and in life.

The course group should have a policy upholding equal opportunities and will work within the policy of the college. In addition there should be encouragement for all-female or all-black or all-male support groups if this is what the students find helpful.

It is notable that when a particular group is represented in a staff team, that particular grouping among the students is increased. The move to have staff teams that mirror the society in which we live is an important trend in counselling training and a way of supporting self-direction for groups who, so far, have not had this experience.

While it can be comparatively easy to challange overt racism or heterosexism it is difficult for a group of staff and students to retain a constant awareness of the bias within the counselling model itself. This makes it difficult to reach a clear coherent policy and well-thought-out structures for clarifying, challenging and changing this bias. Staff can at least address the bias, teach about oppression and the oppressive nature of institutions. Part of their staff development time can be spent addressing prejudice among themselves. This should help them to support the students to interpret the Equal Opportunities legislation in a way that does not undermine self-direction and to take useful direct action when they are clear what that action should be.

It has been moving to watch large groups struggle to work with issues of oppression, to watch the consternation on the faces of white students when black students declare their overriding need to work in a black group with a black facilitator, or to watch male or heterosexual students realize that they have been unawarely sexist or heterosexist. And of course sometimes this awareness does not dawn. Is this the time for sledgehammer tactics? Or should members of the course community simply accept people as they are, in the expectation that if they can be fully heard and attended to they will change? How does the latter approach marry with a college policy that states that racist remarks should always be challenged?

Some strategies that have been found to be useful are:

- helping white students become aware of the significance of being white in a multi-racial society
- engaging non-combatively with people who make oppressive remarks
- accepting and exploring the bias within counselling
- highlighting this without colluding with it
- confronting the potential political nature of counselling

- during counselling skills practice, making sure that the culture, background and personal history of the client and counsellor are acknowledged
- offering teaching on the nature of oppression
- highlighting oppressive circumstances as they occur in the group
- including useful booklists and references to research on subject areas relating to equal opportunities in pre-course material and at the end of workshops
- highlighting issues of power in one-to-one and group relations and offering support to people who feel less powerful in a particular relationship.

Staff should take the lead in highlighting the oppressive possibilities in any group. They must also hear students when they talk about this and support them in being aware of ways in which they experience oppression and are oppressive.

SUPPORTING SELF-DIRECTED LEARNING

Most self-directing learners, while they will rebel against support at times, will welcome clear suggestions about ways to deepen their understanding of counselling.

Ways of enhancing the students' self-direction in counsellor training include:

1 Ask students to engage in counselling as a client while they are in training.
2 Run workshops where the theoretical aspects of a model are supported by students working together to experience and demonstrate the techniques involved.
3 Use a large number of exercises where people have the opportunity to become clients. This personal material is seen as a valuable learning resource. The ground rules and later the Community Contract aim to provide safety and respect for this highly personal learning resource.
4 Form small groups where people focus on their own personal development and learning. These groups are encouraged to feed back in some way to others in the learning group.
5 Have staff offer comments in the large group which illustrate the way primitive defence mechanisms can manifest themselves and affect the workings of any large group or organization. Students are encouraged to transfer this learning to their own organizations and to think about how they can use their theoretical and practical knowledge to encourage change in their organizations.
6 Make connections between the processes that occur in the large group

and the processes that occur in counselling. As mechanisms such as projection and projective identification become clarified in the large group and theoretical material is made available, students are in a better position to identify and define current powerful and often distressing experiences.

A student had this to say about the experience of understanding projection in the large course group:

> There was an issue of power in the group, and I think we all got stuck to some extent in particular roles, giving power to a few and complaining about feeling powerless! I know that when some information about projective identification in groups was given out this helped me to unstick myself and begin to grow in the large group! I was able to acknowledge who I was and how I felt, and shared this in the group.

The students had the experience, took time to reflect on it, were offered theoretical material about projection and then asked to relate that to what happened to them and encouraged to understand it for themselves. They then tried out new behaviour in the group in the light of their subjective experience and increased theoretical understanding.

7 Encourage students to notice the effect of moving between the different roles required of them in self-directed learning, e.g. group facilitator, friend, peer, counsellor and client. Through taking on different roles students learn not to collude with each other. Whereas a friend might support another student in defending herself against the idea that she is a poor listener, someone playing the role of counsellor or observer will feel obliged to point this out, particularly as she may later be assessing this person.

8 Expect that for part of the week the student will be in work which involves counselling and/or the use of counselling skills, and on the course (which is part-time) encourage her to form learning plans which will support her professional development at work.

9 Make the experience of past students available to present students. This is done at selection (see Chapter 4). Occasionally ex-students want to come back and talk about their experience with present students. Staff will also be able to give an account of past events, and make available written material by past students (with their permission).

10 Use supervisors whose knowledge and experience of self-directed learning helps students use the course productively.

11 Support and encourage regular review so that students can assess whether or not the contract and the learning plans they have made do genuinely support their needs and wants.

Even with support, a number of difficulties arise which perhaps can never be fully resolved. However, staff can remain actively engaged with the constant dilemma of how much to offer and how much to hold back.

HOW SELF-DIRECTED LEARNING CAN GO WRONG AND WHAT TO DO

There are a number of possible dilemmas within self-directed learning. One is that of leading people towards self-direction! A metaphor that presents itself is that of helping a rock or boulder fulfil natural laws and nudge its way gently down a slope. Occasionally, perhaps, the boulder will stick in a crevice and a little tap, or at the most, a gentle shove will be needed to help it use its own energy and the facilities in the environment to progress.

When all is working well, a group sees the natural way to go and welcomes onward encouragement. In such a partnership between staff and students, both recognize an end point, a direction and the need to work together.

In less felicitous circumstances the goals get lost or there are deep disagreements about how to reach them. Both sides emerge angry and frustrated and at the worst with a strong desire to direct or control others.

The staff need to think about how they can best fulfil their facilitative role. They will each have their own view of when and how to intervene. The main consideration should be how they can position themselves so that a light tap will set the boulder on its way, rather than finding themselves trying to push an enormous boulder to the top of a steep slope.

The staff learn how to be strongly present without necessarily leading. They might ask questions like

- What would be a useful next step?
- Who should take it?
- How can this step be taken?
- How long have we got before we need to move on to the next stage?
- Who is doing most of the talking in this group?
- How are decisions taken?
- Who gets their own way most of the time?

This method of questioning ensures that the staff's influence is mainly on the method of planning a timetable or a programme for learning rather than on the content. They are sharing an inquiry rather than telling or teaching. They are also focusing on the students' ability to take things further.

Another way of focusing the students or sharing the inquiry with them is by making summative statements. For example, sometimes a tired group will be ready to accept a simplistic solution or decision from an influential group member. A statement like 'Well, that would be one possible course of action' will offer time to consider both the fulfilment of the task and the operation of the group process during its fulfilment.

The basic counselling skills of summarizing, paraphrasing or reflecting can be used in a large group and will allow the space for reflection that can illuminate action and feeling.

Staff will know that there are pitfalls like arriving at unreal solutions and not facing up to genuine learning needs. They also know from their experiences that difficult experiences like conflict can be overcome. They are there to help students acquire appropriate aims and face the difficulties involved in achieving them, to decide when a thing should be left or pursued, to notice the power of wishful thinking or of unreal solutions. They will be aware of the difficulties caused by over-anxiety or of anxiety-denying behaviour.

It will be important to the students that the staff do not let themselves be pushed into the roles of messiah delivering them to a mythical promised land, or of mother goddess or earth mother, offering the solution to feelings of deprivation. The students' feelings of loss and anger later when the superhuman figure is found to be less than perfect are great, and sometimes very difficult for a harassed member of staff to bear.

Although the staff may have less formal power than on conventional courses, at a personal level they are likely to have a great deal, and it is important that this is acknowledged. Choices about which model of counselling to learn about may well be made on the basis of a transferential relationship to a member of staff. There should be a common understanding about the nature of transference and how to deal with it. Having accepted that transference will occur, the staff member can be circumspect in the way she deals with it.

As the staff member develops her skill she is able to choose quickly from a spectrum of methods of interaction the appropriate one for a particular student at a particular time.

She is able to teach students to negotiate and co-operate and encourage them to be responsible and participative as learners. She works from some basic values which include encouraging people to arrive at their own system of values and that everyone's value system is usually given equal respect.

A model such as John Heron's six-category interventions (Heron, 1986; see pp. 20–1 above) is helpful to ensure that a range of suitable interventions is available from a staff team. For example, it is important to have staff who can confront the students effectively as well as having people who make mainly cathartic or informative interventions.

At times the contradictions within the staff role will confuse both staff and students. For example, despite careful preparation some students may well still expect staff to lead from the front and issue a timetable and a preset schedule of work. Others in the employing institution may expect the same.

The staff will judge that the greater wisdom lies in restraint and that the students will discover their way forward for themselves. If the students do not fully understand this they may well feel abandoned and become distressed or rebellious. When this happens they will need to be heard, respected, attended to and reminded about boundaries. The skill, management and judgement required for these decisions may well go unrecognized and this, in times of stress, tension and diminishing resources, adds the further stress of role conflict and demoralization. The staff should be strong and supported by each other. It is also important that in doing so and in taking care of the boundaries of the course they do not appear to be withholding knowledge, information or care from the students.

Staff should agree about basic values. It is helpful for all concerned if there is a central core and a unified position from which to help the students assess their learning needs. Differences in style and method are useful but there should be a shared belief system and a unified approach in dealing with the students. Exposure to the different models of counselling used by different staff members will be useful to students in that it tends to throw them back on their own resources and encourage them to make choices about the models and ideas they wish to follow. However, it can be confusing if there is no clear teaching or explanation about the differences.

One of the most easily made mistakes is that of abandoning the hierarchical method too early. This can leave the students feeling unsafe, panicky and ultimately quite hostile towards the staff. The staff and students will need to take time sharing responsibility for the management of the learning group and, after this has been working successfully for a time, the staff can move further into the background leaving the students with most of the responsibility. Staff are still there to offer support, evaluation and challenge. Of central importance to self-directed learning is goodwill towards it as a process from all those participating in the course. The system is quite vulnerable to attack. There may be a sub-group of students who do not want the organization to function effectively. It can be very difficult to work constructively if such a sub-group cannot be challenged and contained.

An unsupportive and destructive climate can develop if the students feel unsafe in the early stages. They must receive effective preparation for this style of learning. The energy and motivation that made them apply for this type of course must be nourished and not destroyed. If group members loose their goodwill through fear, or because they do not experience being heard or acknowledged, the process is sabotaged. A group of students who are angry because they are personally insecure or uncertain about the method can be quite destructive. They can undermine the staff's role and discourage co-operative learning. This can be a very difficult situation to retrieve and it is best to prevent it happening by ensuring that the students feel secure and 'held' from the start. Successful induction weekends are well structured and tightly held by the staff team but still succeed in leading people towards self-direction (see Chapter 4, pp. 60–1 for a sample timetable).

Staff need to be confident that they can create a good learning environment and should do so. They cannot do so unless there is a readiness and a preparedness within the students for this kind of learning and the hazards and challenges and excitement involved.

The intention throughout this chapter has been to consider some of the important issues and challenges in self-directed learning. It concludes Part One. Part Two is concerned with operational aspects. The next chapter provides a framework by means of which this method of learning can be facilitated. It offers concrete examples of ways of preparing the students and of providing a helpful induction. It also looks at the tasks and achievements of each year of the course.

PART TWO

Self-directed learning in action in counsellor training

Chapters 4, 5 and 6 are concerned with the operational aspects of self-directed learning. Chapter 4 offers a framework for the use of self-directed learning in counsellor training. Chapter 5 details the tasks involved in forming a learning group and taking it through to the final assessment. Chapter 6 discusses supervision as a support to self-directed learning.

FOUR

Creating a framework

This chapter is concerned with the framework which supports the work of building a self-directed course. It looks at preparation, induction and the use of contracts, which are seen as essential supports to self-directed learning, providing a framework on which the counselling course can be constructed.

THE FRAMEWORK FOR SELF-DIRECTED LEARNING

Comprehensive preparation, careful induction and effective use of learning contracts provide the structure on which students, aided by the staff, can build a counselling course which is in tune with their needs as people and as counsellors.

This chapter together with Chapter 5 provides a demonstration of one way to put self-directed learning in counselling training into action. The example is based on the courses that ran at Southwark and South West London Colleges, using these courses to demonstrate a method of working. It is not intended to be an accurate or historical account, although most of the material used is based on the author's experience as a member of staff on both courses.

The counselling courses at South West London College began in the early 1970s. In their original form they offered a very basic skills training to people such as clergy, doctors, welfare officers, student counsellors, Further Education lecturers, school teachers and playgroup leaders, who felt they needed to use counselling skills in their work. As their reputation spread and its scope widened they also offered a qualification to people who wanted to take up counselling as a full-time career. Influenced by the spirit of the times and by the energy and skills of the staff, the teaching method evolved from being staff-led to one in which self-directed learning and self and peer assessment were the central features. The staff soon realized that self-directed learning cannot be put into action without a very secure framework to support it. This framework is made up of a carefully designed preparatory stage, followed by an intensive introduction and some very clear contracting about the relationship between the students and the college. During the course the students must have clear agreements among themselves about the learning that is to be done and how it is to be done.

Self-directed learning has had a formative influence on counselling training. In the 1970s the main tenets were seen by many as highly innovatory, challenging or even outrageous. Now many courses attempt to encourage a self-directed element. They invite their students to offer feedback, work in a large group, produce a portfolio and engage in self and peer assessment. Few, if any, offer their students a free choice over the content of timetables or accept that the qualification should be awarded without any staff assessment. Some courses profess to offer a self-directed element by leaving the students to plan a few guest lectures while the rest of the course is highly structured and planned in advance by the staff. This may be a useful activity but should not be equated with allowing students to find their own direction in learning.

Our model is of a three-year part-time course comprising a basic foundation year followed by a two-year diploma course. The model incorporates distinct stages of growth and moves from the foundation stage, in which students are introduced to the ideas of self-direction, to the two-year diploma course, in which the focus is on working together as a learning organization in order to achieve a clear contract that will enable self and peer assessment to happen. The course takes place on one day a week and for the rest of the week students are expected to be in work, either paid or voluntary, which involves the use of counselling or counselling skills.

Self-directed learning requires thoughtful preparation and induction. Students are required to be clear what they are committing themselves to when they embark on a course that offers a training in counselling. Furthermore, they should be aware of what is meant by self-directed learning in this context and of its implications. They should realize that they will be held responsible for what and how they learn; that they will be involved in what and how others learn. They should make working agreements about how this learning takes place and be clear about the standards they require of themselves and each other in order to provide a good service to clients. They will need to be able to communicate directly to each other about those standards and find ways of assessing themselves and each other. The course is not provided for them; rather, they create and build it for themselves.

The framework for self-directed learning consists of giving students suitable preparation and introduction and a clear contract with the college or awarding body. Students strengthen this framework firstly by drawing up a personal contract which includes a learning plan and sets out their aims and objectives. Secondly, they work with the other students to create a Community Contract or joint statement about how they will work together and what they intend to achieve as a group. They now have some fixed points within which they work for and achieve self direction.

The next three sections of this chapter consider:

- how to prepare students for self-directed learning
- how to introduce the students to the ideas and experiences involved in self-directed learning
- how to make clear working agreements or contracts that will support that learning.

PREPARATION

An effective way to prepare students for self-directed learning is to offer them the means to think about the method in advance. Students can be given an induction pack before they come on the course. This can contain a work-sheet, reading list, course manual, and course brochure.

The work-sheet will direct the student towards the brochure and the essential course requirements. For example, is the student doing counselling as part of her work? Is she doing enough counselling to benefit from this particular course? Has she enough self-awareness, skills and knowledge to help others learn from the course? Does she know what 'self-directed' means? It is also intended to help her consider the meaning of self-directed learning by asking questions such as

- Can you envisage working in a self-directed community?
- What would that involve?
- Why are you attracted to the course?
- What are your perceptions of the way it works?
- What would your learning goals be in the foundation year?
- Are there resources to meet these?
- What can you offer the learning community?
- Does this learning model make sense?
- What further clarification do you need?

The student is asked to complete the work-sheet before coming to a self-selection workshop and bring it with her so that she can use the resources provided by the workshop to answer her own questions. Access to the course tutor should be easily available if she needs clarification concerning the questions, the workshop, or entrance requirements.

The brochure sets out the aims and methodology, course requirements, qualifications needed and qualification offered. Other important aids are a reading list similar to the one available at the end of this book, and a course manual which can be used to illuminate different aspects of the course. The manual will contain very practical information but will also give some guidance on the connection between a self-directed course and counselling skills, managing learning as an individual and in a community, the function of the residential courses, setting up the machinery for self and peer assessment.

As well as this preliminary written material, students should have an active participatory experience of this type of learning before formally applying for the course. This will happen at the self-selection workshop and will help them decide whether or not the course is right for them.

At the self-selection workshop, staff give a short but clear definition of self-directed learning, generally along the lines of:

> This type of learning is focused on the person and her needs. We aim to help the student discover what she wants to learn about counselling. We also help her to think about the ways in which she wants to develop as a person. Someone who is learning and developing is likely to be able to help others to learn with her in a co-operative group and be an inspiring counsellor for her clients. We as staff want you to learn from your experience and we are here to help you do that. We do not know what you need to learn but will offer suggestions and exercises which are intended to help you get in touch with your needs.

The staff describe themselves as an important learning resource and they also indicate the many other resources such as books, hand-outs, tapes, computers, video recorders and the other important human resource, the other students. They may suggest other forms of preparation for the course such as reading *Freedom to Learn* by Carl Rogers (Rogers, 1994), attending suitable workshops, meeting as many ex-students as possible, finding out about other colleges' courses which use a comparable method of learning, for example North East London University's School for Independent Study.

There are generally some questions about the amount of counselling students should be doing. Current students can help here by describing their work settings and the way they have used at work what they learned on the course. The staff also point out that supervision in the diploma years will require case presentation so that the students should be doing enough work to provide material for supervision.

The workshop should be designed to help people ask useful questions and find some answers. It is helpful to have current students involved in the organization of the event, to have hand-outs and samples of students' work available, and visual aids pinned on the wall providing further information. The workshop should convey something of the feeling, atmosphere and ideology of the course.

A self-selection workshop could have roughly this format:

Prospective students are welcomed and given an introduction to the programme, which falls into three parts:

(1) Information giving

In the information-giving part, reference can be made to the course brochure. The course objectives are set out and there is some discussion about the way the course content and format are intended to meet the course objectives. Students are told that the courses are self-directed learning communities with the emphasis on learning about counselling and counselling skills.

As a way of allowing prospective students to sample one of the methods used on the course staff running the workshop might offer a guided fantasy, perhaps taking people on an imaginary journey and getting them to visualize their first few days on the course or the introductory weekend. This helps people begin to think about what they want from such a course. It also gives a clear message about the student's participative role in her own learning. The students' experience of the visualization and their comments and contributions are later fed into a plenary session and it is made clear that their feedback will be taken into account.

(2) Discussion in small groups

Time is allowed for people to debrief in pairs and then small groups and then notice what questions they still need answering. These can be dealt with by a member of staff and a present student in each group.

(3) Plenary session for questions and recapitulation of essential information

There is a final plenary for giving information concerning dates and fees, and for any comments or feedback on the evening.

Students make a formal application after they have been to the self-selection workshop and after it has been ascertained that they have the necessary qualifications and experience to be considered for entry. They will be expected to be at least 25 years old, have A level or the equivalent and to be in work which involves the use of counselling skills. They will now fill in an application form on which there are a number of questions designed to help people demonstrate what they mean by self-directed learning. Students self-select and the staff make a final decision ensuring that people have the basic entry qualifications and that there is a well-balanced mixture of people on the course.

This preliminary work needs to be followed up by an intensive induction after students join the course; the intention here is to help the students approach self-directed learning with as much clear information as possible about what is expected from them.

INTRODUCING STUDENTS TO SELF-DIRECTED LEARNING

Once the students have been accepted they are invited to an introductory residential planning weekend. The way the weekend is organized and the activities it contains illustrate self-direction. The purpose is first to discover and acknowledge learning needs; then to recognize and manage the resources available; and finally to organize collectively a programme for the forthcoming term. Other purposes are to begin to form as a group and to grasp the spirit and essence of self-direction. In addition, students will have personal agendas concerning what they want to learn, the skills they wish to develop and personal needs and will want to test the ground to see if these can be accommodated.

During the first session structures are offered to help people get to know one another. Students form temporary groups and are encouraged to express hopes and fears about the weekend. The next day, after re-forming as a group, objectives are listed and people are asked to think about and say what they want to achieve by the end of the year.

An exercise called 'Lifeline' is often used. During this exercise students work on their own for a time. They draw a line which represents their life and on which they chart major turning points or significant life events. When they talk about this later with others they gain the opportunity for greater understanding of how different events have affected their development. They are encourage to dwell on particular stages, describe events, feel the sensations, and reassess and re-evaluate the effect of those experiences. Some of their unconscious wishes and needs begin to surface. This material needs to be processed, i.e. worked with, listened to, support offered, meaning given. Time is required to work carefully with such material and it can be useful to have a long break on the afternoon of the second day for rest, recreation and recuperation. This level of work is exhausting and staff and students must rest and recharge.

After this exercise, which is generally quite powerful in its effect, students are asked to start considering what they need to learn now and in the future. For example, someone who experienced violence as a child would need time to understand how this has affected her as an adult and to decide whether she can use her experience helpfully to benefit others. The students talk about this in small groups and become aware of the personal resources they have used in dealing with some of these events.

They become clearer about the ways that major events have influenced their lives. They notice how they have learned to cope with loss and change. As well as coming to grips with their needs they also notice the skills and talents which have brought them this far.

This exercise brings up different needs and objectives and it becomes clear that the timetable will not be based purely on intellectual needs. Staff and students realize that the world of feeling must have its place in planning learning. The facilitators aim to acknowledge this dimension and to produce structures and exercises which accommodate emotional as well as intellectual needs.

Later an exercise is devised to match needs and resources. People display an interest, perhaps using a placard, and walk about finding others to join them. They talk about what they want to learn and how they want to learn about that particular subject, for example family dynamics, and then look for others with similar interests, changing and adapting their aims as they go, making use of the interactions to find out more about their fellow students and enjoying the experience of meeting people who are interested in the same things or perhaps have had similar life experiences to themselves. As they discuss their plans for the term, students devise interesting and innovative ways of accommodating both cognitive and affective learning needs.

For example, they may wish to learn more about family dynamics by bringing photographs of themselves as children, talking about childhood experiences, linking these to how they are now, forming their own theories as well as studying those of others.

Staff encourage students to prioritize their learning needs. Information is given about available resources and the students finally decide on their most important learning need, find others with compatible needs and negotiate for resources and to get their choices on the timetable. Some course groups will find it very important to produce a timetable. Others, even at the foundation stage, have seemed much more interested in emphasizing the emotional needs of the group, in examining interactions, and are not particularly focused on the timetable at this point. Appendix 1 (pp. 105–6) contains examples of other kinds of exercises which can facilitate these introductory weekends.

The location of the residential weekend is important. Taking the student group away to a pleasant environment where they are freed from normal domestic and professional commitments allows them to focus on the first stages of formation as a group and offers the staff an opportunity to provide an intensive introduction to a self-directed way of working and learning as well as beginning to plan a timetable within the fixed points and overall objectives of the course.

Staff facilitate this in the following ways:

• by providing a programme for the weekend

- by providing safety
- by offering attention
- by providing boundaries
- by not doing too much for students
- by varying the programme at times to meet needs as they arise
- by sticking to the programme where it appears to be meeting the needs of the group
- by doing a considerable amount of planning in advance including being sensitive and supportive to each other's professional and personal needs and requirements
- by encouraging the group to form its own ground rules which aid direct communication, for example, speaking in the first person rather than generalizing.

Given this induction and facilitation the group will quickly create its own culture and identity and the new surroundings and different stimuli will encourage some questioning of previous habits and patterns.

These introductory weekends invariably make a profound impression on the attenders, who come with a variety of overt and covert needs. Some students come in the hope of making alliances and friendships. These may well not happen. It is more likely that they will be strongly challenged about their habitual methods of communicating and will need to think again about some of their assumptions about others.

Other students may want to see a very definite timetable, modelled on conventional lines with the staff firmly in control. Some students may want a theoretical approach and may be unhappy in practice with the continued emphasis on their experience and personal responsibility. Other students may want to see more emphasis on providing equal opportunities for minority groups and be disappointed by the white middle-class composition of the staff and student groups. Some people may be quite terrified by the apparent lack of structure and be totally unable to remember the rationale for the lack of a given syllabus or timetable. Other students may have been consciously and/or unconsciously working towards just such an educational opportunity and feel immediately at ease in the environment that is offered.

One student said of her first introductory weekend 'I was exactly where I wanted to be at exactly the time I wanted to be there'. Her personal and professional development had prepared her to take responsibility for her needs and wants and to find and create opportunities and processes wherein these would be met. A self-directed course offered her the opportunity to meet her needs as a professional and as a person and to carry on exercising personal autonomy and responsibility.

Another student said:

We established ourselves as a community. There seemed to be a community spirit. We were there to work out what our tasks needed to be. I learned a lot about the way people use language and the effect that has. I learned to distinguish between think and feel. I learned to 'own' what I said and not to speak for other people. Mainly I learned this by staff and students pointing it out in the large group when engaged in the task of planning community learning.

Courses in the 1990s battle against severe financial constraints. However, it is nevertheless important to have access to sufficient resources to provide an intense experience at the beginning of a course with determined direction from the staff. They provide a clear timetable for the weekend. They introduce themselves and the course by giving information about both, and they encourage the students to get to know each other by providing ice-breakers and name games at the beginning. They offer exercises. They take great pains through the use of guided fantasy and other group exercises to help the students become aware of the difference between this educational opportunity and some of the educational experiences they have had in the past, and they prepare themselves to act as counsellors and mentors to help the students understand the different expectations that are being laid on them. The staff should provide boundaries which allow and encourage experimentation with what the concept of self-direction can mean for particular individuals in their personal and working lives. Staff will also wish to convey the sense that the students can have much control and influence on their course of training.

The same student also says of the weekend:

I learned a lot about communication. Things were on a different level. More direct. Communication got very clear very quickly. People tried to get to what was said and meant, very exciting. There was some seminal learning on Group Dynamics – exclusion and inclusion issues were to the fore. I was thinking about where to make my alliances, to find people I could feel safe with. These needs were not fully met. I felt alone some of the time. There was almost too much to learn! So many condensed human experiences. I was energized by the personal learning and by the group processes.

The students and staff co-operate to plan the course, using organic and symbolic methods to find out what people want and need, coping as a group with the fact that not everyone will get what they want and still striving to create an equitable system. This means that the staff, and indeed also the students, will be watchful of the group dynamics and monitor tendencies to rescue and persecute. Because these things are being observed at a time when people's energies are focused on achieving a task, they become live issues rather than merely concepts read about in books. People can see being enacted in front of them tendencies which can help or hinder a group in its task. They feel deprived, excluded or invaded as well as triumphant, greedy and competitive. They need to learn to handle these feelings or risk failing in the task of co-operative community-based learning. This leaves them with images, sounds and sensations that can last a lifetime. Theories about groups come alive when the ideas become a visible and audible reality.

By the end of the introductory weekend students will have learned a great deal about group formation, a considerable amount about each other and what happens in large groups. They will have had an initial ex-perience of working co-operatively and of starting to manage their own learning. They may have produced a timetable for the first term; an example is given here.

2.00 – 2.10 pm	General announcements
2.15 – 3.45 pm	Workshops on:
	counselling skills, or
	person-centred counselling, or
	family dynamics, or
	working with anger
3.45 – 4.15 pm	Tea break
4.15 – 5.30 pm	Large Group Meeting on a stated topic such as eval-uation, planning the next term's timetable, or to study the large group.
5.30 – 7.00 pm	Personal development groups

Students will have been introduced to the idea of making contracts about learning and will have become clearer about the contract they have entered into with each other and with the college.

CONTRACTS OR WORKING AGREEMENTS IN SELF-DIRECTED LEARNING

On a self-directed course it would be easy for students continually to move the goalposts and never formally account for their learning. However, people have come on the course in order to learn about coun-selling and they are asked to take responsibility for recording their progress to themselves and each other.

Contracts are set up in order to help people be accountable while on the course. They are set up to provide the student with some security and to uphold the principle of self-responsibility within an atmosphere of freedom. The contracts that are laid down in advance should be clearly set out in both the course brochure and the student manual. Those made on the course will be included in the portfolio.

When students elect to learn about counselling through self-directed learning they enter into a carefully constructed contract with the college or university to which the course belongs. The contract they take on is designed by the counselling course staff and falls into three parts.

Part 1 concerns entry, counselling activity while on the course, and attendance. The student is expected to attend regularly and be engaged in counselling in some way for the duration of the course.

Part 2 concerns self-directed learning. Students and staff undertake to plan a suitable programme which will provide a safe and stimulating environment for people to learn about self-direction and to carry it out.

Part 3 concerns self and peer assessment and the eventual award of the diploma. The students must accept these responsibilities and work with others to carry them out.

In order to support parts 2 and 3 of their overall contract with the college, students create a personal learning contract which sets out their individual aims and objectives for the year and contains a learning plan and a Large Group or Community Contract which sets out the way they intend to work together, ground rules, and, eventually, a structure for self and peer assessment. Students may well start to set up their personal learning contracts on the introductory weekend and these are reviewed and changed regularly throughout the three years. Peer assessment of the portfolios uses the personal contract as a yardstick for assessment. Work on the Community Contract begins in the first year of the diploma course.

EXAMPLE OF A PERSONAL CONTRACT

I want to grow and develop, to stretch myself at times and learn to be more positive and confident, also to become more assertive and learn different skills, to trust my own sense of what is right for me, have a strong sense of who I am, what I want and to own it, as well as learning to deal with confrontation in a non-threatening way. I would like to find support for these aims within my small group where we intend to practise skills and give feedback. I would also like to ensure that I work with particular members of staff whom I see as having many of these skills.

More specifically I want to experience workshops in Gestalt and Rogerian Therapy so that I can use these methods in my work. I want to practise using two-chair work as I feel inhibited in working in this way at the moment.

A contract is a working agreement about how a task is to be carried out in order to reach specific goals. In self-directed and experiential learning the personal learning contract creates structure and form and enables the learner to be aware of what she wants to learn and, later, to find out whether or not she has learned it. She can plan what she can learn further. The contract gives concreteness and specificity to her learning and is a bridge between her inner hopes and fears and what she can expect to achieve in reality.

Work on the Community Contract begins towards the end of the foundation year and is usually completed sometime during the first year of the diploma course. It is like a manifesto, and also a statement of norms and values, perhaps a map of the territory as far as it is known. It is also a working agreement about how members of the learning community will co–operate in order to carry out their joint tasks. As assessment approaches it will be sharpened up into a statement of what is to be done, how and by whom and when it will be done and will include a timetable and structure for assessment.

EXAMPLE OF A COMMUNITY CONTRACT

There will be a commitment regarding attendance and submission of set work e.g. minimum of 75 per cent attendance and submission of all set work by the deadlines.

The group will work in such a way that support, feedback and challenge are given.

Reservations about people's work and use of counselling skills or under-standing and interpretation of the counselling process are communicated respectfully well before the deadline for submission for portfolios.

All students provide evidence of being able to work within at least one core theoretical model.

Students think about their counselling philosophy and are able to make a statement about this.

Students show that they have worked for a reasonable length of time with more than one client.

Students demonstrate personal growth, self-awareness, and self-evaluation in line with their personal contracts.

Students devise suitable methods for monitoring and assessment.

Students agree to work within the college policies regarding equal opportunities and look for ways in which the principles behind the policies are compatible with self-direction and counselling.

Later a statement about how the final assessment will be carried out will be added to this in line with the original commitment to the college to self and peer assess (see Chapter 2, p. 25).

Developing a Community Contract brings the learning group together and focuses it on finding and defining its identity. Its completion marks an important life stage in any course group. The community contract is an extension of the basic ground rules which students and staff construct at the original introductory planning weekend. It sets out the values of the group of learners, what it sees as good counselling and how it intends to assess the evidence of counselling skills. Creating this working agreement is a formative experience in the life of a course community. The group spends some time developing it, and it will be revised and discussed a great deal. There will be many differing norms and values within the group and the aim will be to reach a consensus so that everyone's norms and values are represented in some way. There are generally fierce arguments about, for example, equal opportunities and how these can be supported in counselling and in assessment of counsellors and their skills; counselling as a method of political control; how much counselling people should be doing; the role of the staff; what counselling is; and the need for a core theoretical model and philosophical statement.

As students become more adept at using the large group to study the way organizations function they begin to notice and question the way decisions are made. As so often happens within organizations, many decisions seem to 'get themselves' made. Nobody is quite sure how or when this happened but somehow certain traditions arise and are not questioned. These can range from the trivial, such as tea at 4.00, to something profoundly important, such as never confronting a black person in the large group or deferring to one particular person or group of people more than another. Sooner or later it is noticed that decisions all too often are made 'accidentally', perhaps as a result of an unconscious wish to avoid honest dissent. In a group where there has been a great deal of destructive conflict a few people may quite consciously decide to push an important decision through. Such individuals may have decided that they know how to 'work' the large group and be quite efficient at carrying out some important decision-making. The rest of the group may be so tired of dissent that they will let them. However it is fairly easy to predict that when individuals regain their energy they will, if they think they have been insufficiently consulted, sabotage attempts to move the group forward. While it is not necessary to provoke or create conflict its acceptance as part of group living can help take away some of the fears which surround it. Through engaging in exercises such as the following, course groups can accept conflict as something to be worked with rather than shunned.

EXAMPLE OF AN EXERCISE AIMED AT CONFLICT RESOLUTION AND CONSENSUS

> Four or five facilitators, possibly a mixture of staff and students, run the exercise, which is for the whole group and takes at least three hours. There is an introductory statement about how the exercise is to be run with a reminder about ground rules.

> 1. Students work on their own allowing their feelings and thoughts about conflict to surface. They are asked to remember early childhood and think back to their first experiences of conflict. They will remember what this was like, what their feelings were, what attempts were made towards resolution. They can consider how this affected them as an individual and also the effect on their families. There may be a guided visualization. They may be encouraged to draw

or write about their feelings. They will be asked to consider how they handle conflict now. What feelings are evoked in them at the sound of angry voices?

People are then given the opportunity to talk about this experience in private with one or two others. Some of this material may be aired in the large group. Later it may be taken to supervision or personal counselling.

The students are listened to with respect. Time is taken to make sure that people are heard and attended to. The group is asked whether or not they are willing to go on and work towards conflict resolution. If so, the facilitators are given a mandate to continue to work with the group to find a way to help them work through conflict towards consensus.

2. The conflict is defined.
For example, there may be a considerable amount of disagreement over whether students should decide for themselves what to put in the portfolio, or the contents be laid down in advance by the learning community.

3. People say what they feel and think about the problem.
A considerable amount of time and attention is devoted to this. Those who do not speak easily are invited to give their opinions and there are frequent short sessions in pairs or very small groups where time and attention is given to individual difficulties. People may be asked to raise their hands to indicate their views on various aspects of the problem. This is taken as an opinion picture and the facilitators try to find ways to accommodate the views of the minority as well as the majority.

When it is clear that people experience themselves as being heard and accepted it is proposed that the group moves on to the solution-seeking stage.

4. There is a group brainstorm.
Again, this phase should not be rushed. Sensible and wild solutions should be written up on large sheets of paper and left for all to see. The group may decide to adjourn to let ideas take root and to have rest or refreshment. Facilitators should check that everyone feels that their ideas have been taken account of and recorded, not just those who are most articulate or have the loudest voices.

5. Proposals for a solution are made.
This can be done by using a small group to categorize and prioritize items on the brainstorm, make proposals and check for agreement. Some time is spent discussing, arguing, compromising, accepting and respecting the views of the minority. A solution is not settled upon until students feel sufficiently heard and understood to accept a view that is not theirs but contains enough important material to be useful to the group as a whole.

6. There is an evaluation and feedback session.
Some time is spent checking how people whose views did not prevail are

feeling, offering support and continuing to think about ways in which their needs can be respected.

The facilitators are thanked and appreciated for their work. They are also given feedback on the different part of the exercises and are told what worked or did not work.

7. The group celebrate their achievement.
   Students are encouraged to realize that they have taken part in a difficult exercise which could have far reaching implications. They can take credit for this, enjoy the result and think about how these ideas can be used elsewhere, perhaps in their work settings or with a local community group.

During the ensuing term there are likely to be a number of community workshops aimed at clarifying the norms and values of the group. The results of these will affect the final version of the Community Contract and will offer important guidelines for the construction of an effective assessment system. Again, this is done through a series of community workshops, often facilitated by students or by small working parties of students and staff. During these workshops people will be encouraged to make explicit their values, think about what they are aiming to do when counselling, be clear about minimum requirements and begin to think about how these could be applied.

For example, in a workshop aimed to help students become clearer about their values they are asked to think about their values, how they arrived at them, what they are. They do this first on their own, write their conclusions down and then show them to others in a small group. People think about their most cherished values and how they act on them, and are asked to think about how they act on them on the course. Broad areas such as justice, confidentiality, doing good rather than harm, honesty and autonomy are some of the values people speak about.

Students can be asked to consider a number of questions in order to help them decide on a common statement:

- How do they act on their values?
- How do they betray them, in their lives, in the course group?
- What relevance do these values have in counselling?
- As a client, what values would they want their counsellor to hold to?
- Which values are significant enough to be included in a working agreement between people to support each other's learning and to evaluate each other's ability to work as a counsellor or use counselling skills?

Much of the thinking about this will be done in small groups and then the ideas put together and incorporated into the Community Contract. The Community Contract, together with the individual student's personal learning contract, forms the basis of self and peer assessment.

There is a considerable sense of achievement when groups reach agreement – on one occasion a course member brought in a cake to celebrate the fact that a contract had at last been made. The celebration and relief rightly imply that it is a difficult task for a large group of 60 or more people to decide on their values and beliefs as a community of learners. They will have worked through many difficulties and disagreements in order to reach a consensus. This heightens the sense of achievement and gives hope for the future. The possibility of transferring the learning about conflict resolution and achieving consensus in other disparate groups of people is suddenly there.

Much of the work on the second planning weekend, which takes place at the beginning of the first diploma year, is devoted to coming to grips with obstacles to agreement on a clear contract for the whole group. Many of these obstacles will stem from differences, disagreements and misunderstandings between course members and the challenge is to achieve a way of working co-operatively despite these. Members of the learning group strive to work cleanly with their difficulties so that the assessment process can be a good one.

One student, who said she had joined the course because she thought self and peer assessment would be an easy option, later said it was the most difficult thing she had ever done. She said 'There was nowhere to hide', meaning that the people who were to assess her would be likely to know her extremely well and to know if she was trying to camouflage her weaknesses or exaggerate her strengths.

Staff and students work together to evolve criteria by which equitable judgements can be made. The assessment procedure will involve making decisions on what is to be assessed and making this clear to the whole group of staff and students and to the external assessors.

There are a number of key questions. For example, will assessment be confined strictly to what is demonstrated in the portfolio, or will it include what people have seen of each other's work over the last three years? If someone is known to be an impressive or influential speaker in the large group, does that bear a relationship to her counselling skills?

Peer assessors decide what to ask for in order to assess. For example, they may require videos, tapes, detailed written case notes. They must decide what constitutes satisfactory evidence of counselling skills. They must be clear about what it is they need in order to carry out a satisfactory assessment. The Community Contract is the evidence of this clarity.

This chapter has been concerned with setting up the structures which provide an enabling framework or scaffolding. This structure enables the students to design and build the kind of course they need. Chapter 5 describes the different stages of construction in each year of the course. It outlines the tasks and describes the achievements in self-directed learning.

FIVE

Course structure: tasks and achievements in self-directed learning

In Chapter 4 we looked at how a supportive framework is created to allow students to follow their own direction in learning about counselling. As a result of this work they now have a clear starting point and know what they will be responsible for in managing their learning.

There are a number of tasks to be carried out in order to achieve a self-directed training in counselling. These are listed and described below. The tasks and achievements are listed in a particular order but, as will become clear, several of them will be going on at once.

By the beginning of the foundation year students have realized that they must have clear individual learning agendas and find ways of meeting these. The tasks of the first year of the course are aimed at achieving this.

YEAR 1

In year 1 the tasks necessary for self-directed learning are:

- Diagnosing learning needs
- Forming clear objectives
- Finding and using resources
- Learning to work in groups.

Diagnosing learning needs

Students are asked to become clear about what they want and need to learn. In accordance with the principle that people are most likely to get what they want when they are clear what that is, there is an exercise early in the year in which students are asked to list hopes, fears, expectations and wants and needs. They do this first on their own and then discuss these feelings and ideas with one and then several other people. They will be encouraged to think back to the introductory weekend and notice how their thoughts and feelings about learning have changed since then. Eventually joint lists are compiled and put on display. These generally contain items such as:

- Everyone else knows more about counselling than I do. I am afraid that we are going to spend a lot of time sitting in groups being terribly honest with each other.
- I want to be able to express anger constructively and help others do the same.
- I would like to learn about counselling by becoming more fully conscious in my relationships with others on the course.
- I would like to understand my reactions to a recent bereavement so that I can help others in similar circumstances.
- I would like to make new friends.

After examining their hopes and fears, students will then go on to become much more realistic about their learning needs. They are encouraged to discuss them with others. Some people will want to become proficient in one particular model of counselling, for example Gestalt; others may wish to explore the idea of counselling as a method of social control; others may wish to look at how to work with disturbed and disturbing people; others may wish to look at a feature of their own upbringing, for example, having been adopted so that they understand more about the implications when they deal with clients who were adopted.

Usually people start with individual lists, which they share first in small groups and then with the whole group. Despite the mature age of people on a counselling course the atmosphere may well, in part, resemble that of a primary school, as evidenced by the chatter, exclamations, pooling of experiences and making of arrangements to meet during the week to work on something together. The energy of the child is released and is put to use in a number of creative and exciting ways. Above all, it is available to help people learn because what they are to learn is of personal significance to them. They themselves know what they want and need to learn.

Students review some of their formative life experiences. They may do this by working in pairs, by forming personal development groups or by using the Lifeline exercise described in Chapter 4 (p. 60).

A student commented:

I would say that the staff supported self-directed learning in every way. They wouldn't tell you a thing!!! Seriously though! I think we had to struggle a lot with it as a community, and I think the staff had to struggle with us, too, how to enable us to be self-directed. I remember there being huge struggles with task versus process (i.e. some people were very focused on achieving goals, on doing, and others were much more interested in noticing what was happening within and between people on the way to achieving those goals) ... very challenging as a student trying to be self-directed within a community with everyone else struggling to be self-directed too!

These comments highlight the complexity involved in helping people become self-directing. Staff are criticized both for doing too much and for not doing enough. Sometimes they receive warm appreciation for getting it right!

All this is happening at an early stage in the foundation year when people are new to this way of working and are perhaps unsure of the staff and each other. The students, who are predominantly women, are frequently shellshocked by the persistent questions: What do you want? What do you want to do now? Many people find it quite difficult to separate what they do want from what they ought to want. They would much rather help others answer those questions than stay with themselves long enough to even hear the question. This is a very confronting time and some people leave at this point. Some of those leaving are clear that they want a more structured, more didactic course. Others are clear that they do not want this very personal challenge at this time.

However, it is the aim and wish of the staff that people do not leave but allow themselves to experience their authentic selves in a respectful environment. They can be helped to achieve what they want. If they can accept themselves they can allow themselves to experience genuine needs. This self-acceptance can be reinforced by the acceptance of others. It is the essential platform for self-directed learning.

Forming clear objectives

Acknowledging what is wanted and needed is a necessary step towards defining personally relevant objectives. Within the given structure and objectives of the course students must accustom themselves to defining their own objectives and creating individual learning contracts. These objectives are useful if they are concrete, achievable, challenging and relevant. For example, someone working in a women's refuge may wish to understand more about the effects of domestic violence on women and children. She may also want some very practical help in working with the residents and their angry partners. She will need to acknowledge and manage her reactions to violence.

The relatively unstructured environment, taken with the inevitable competitiveness between the students, may well reawaken primitive feelings of, for example, envy, jealousy, anger and sibling rivalry which, as adults, most had suppressed or repressed long ago. Experiencing these feelings and becoming more skilled at handling them in themselves and others will figure in their learning plan as may working with anger (their own and other people's), or using power ethically. Feelings are encouraged, used and accepted to give an added dimension to learning.

Students, of course, may well find themselves achieving a great deal more than their stated objectives. The work they do as a group will give them profound experiences that they could not have predicted and planned for and will often alter their objectives. For example, if they feel intensely competitive with one another they may recall similar feelings in their early family life and wish to ask for a workshop which enables them to examine this more closely. This may lead them to want to learn more about family therapy or family dynamics. This would be with a view to understanding how these feelings are restimulated in the large group and being more skilful when dealing with such issues with clients.

Students discover new aspects of themselves. This can be traumatic and quite confusing. They can be thrown off course and need exercises that will help them clarify their feelings and form learning objectives that are based on genuine needs and wants. Some exercises that have been found helpful are listed below. Staff who are familiar with the relevant models can offer training and/or facilitation.

- The students may work in co-counselling pairs with interventions aimed at 'discharge' i.e. the strong expression of emotion attached to buried hurts which when cleared will lead to a re-evaluation of the experience and a more rational approach to what happens in the present and future. (See Jackins, 1994.)
- The staff's use of interventions from Transactional Analysis helps students to recognize their tendencies to consider their own and others' needs from a Parent or Child ego state rather than from their Adult ego state in a contract between two equals.
- Interventions from the same model will help students recognize their tendencies to Rescue or Persecute. They will be encouraged to recognize these as they happen and given the chance to practise a number of alternative responses and receive feedback. (See Berne, 1964.)
- Virginia Satir's analysis of communication has already been referred to in Chapter 2 (p. 16). It can be used again here to help people begin to understand their tendencies to distract or placate rather than offer level communications. Rather than use their energies trying to manipulate other people's responses they can deepen their awareness of how and when they do this and choose to act differently. They can direct their energy towards achieving objectives which are important for them. (See Satir, 1972.)
- It can be useful to externalize an internal dialogue or argument. One way of doing this would be to ask the student to move between chairs which represent particular states of mind or the different forces

involved in decision-making. She could speak from one chair or state of mind and then move to the other chair to answer herself. This generally frees the student from incessant internal discussions and in this more relaxed state she very often arrives at a solution or resolution. (Perls, 1972.)

It is hoped that these exercises will help people to become clear about some of the irrational forces involved in their decision-making. They are then in a position to form a learning plan that helps them meet their needs for personal development as well as their learning objectives. They will need to consider:

- how they learn (see Chapter 1 for a discussion of Kolb's learning cycle)
- their current strengths and weaknesses and what they will need to do in the future
- how they can measure their learning
- how they might sabotage their learning
- how they might reward themselves while learning
- what they could do if they did not meet their objectives.

Two exercises which have been found helpful at this stage are:

1   The student is asked to remember a good learning experience, to think about its essential ingredients, write some ideas, pictures or symbols on a piece of paper and then pair off and talk with another student about the original experience and her thoughts, feelings and strongest memories. She should spend at least ten minutes describing the experience and saying why it was valuable. The student then listens to her colleague doing the same. They can then be asked to state specifically and clearly what they learned and what was striking about the way they learned it. Both students could then discuss how this affects their present learning experiences on the counselling course.

    Students can again pair up and talk in turn about a negative experience of learning. They can be asked what was the most unpleasant aspect of this and to think how this has affected them since then. Students often talk of very distressing experiences in their early school life and remember being publicly humiliated for some trivial offence at the age of five or six. Needless to say, this has left them deskilled and traumatized in many formal learning situations thereafter.

    Some aspects of the work in pairs can be taken to the large group with a view to developing a common understanding about early experiences in learning.

2   Another useful exercise is to ask students to imagine their favourite teacher and then their worst teacher sitting on the chair opposite them and talk to each in turn about what it was like to be taught by them. They can change chairs and take on the teacher's role and answer back. It is very useful to have other

students and staff witness this and make comments. Plenty of time should be left for students to talk about the exercise and receive support and encouragement. They can be helped to realize and understand what kind of learning experience works well for them and to make sure they get it.

Both the exercises above require skilled facilitation and the availability of support and comfort. They can be highly traumatic for some people. However, by becoming more aware of the roots of their successes and failures in learning students can now make sure that they allow themselves good conditions for further learning. They can use this understanding to construct a workable learning plan which they can use to further their objectives and to ensure that they have the right conditions for learning.

A learning plan may look rather like this:

By the end of the foundation year I would like to:

- become more comfortable at dealing with anger
- understand more about what happens in groups
- become more skilled at working with people from different backgrounds
- gain a deeper understanding of how oppression manifests itself in society
- acquire a working knowledge of at least one model of counselling.

I would like to do this by attending a workshop on anger in which I attempt to become clearer about some of the sources of my discomfort and fear when faced with angry people. I would like the staff and others to focus on group dynamics and comment about them as we work. I would like to be taught about oppression and I would like people to level with me about ways I am oppressive in this group. I would like to attend a series of workshops on Egan so that I can use his three stages to monitor my progress with clients.

I intend to take this learning plan to my small group and ask two people to review it with me at the end of the year. I would like them to challenge me about the things I have not achieved, understand the significance of that and help me work out what I should do about it.

Once the learning plan has been drawn up, the key questions will be:

- Can I put this into practice?
- How do I put it into practice?
- What resources are available to help me do this?

Finding and using resources

In conventional educational situations people will expect resources to be provided. In self-directed learning it is quite plainly stated that some at least of the resources are within the separate individuals who have come to take part in the course. This is particularly so in relation to counselling where despite the use of models and particular techniques and the usual training resources, people will be interested in finding out how to use themselves and their inner experience in order to form a working relationship with their clients. Being a client in their own personal counselling and in exercises on the course will deepen their self-awareness, as will working with others in a personal development group. Healthy constructive feedback from staff and other students will increase their confidence in their own resources.

People's reactions to the statement that they are responsible for their learning are many and diverse. For some, telling them that they already know everything they need to know is like lighting the touch paper. They very quickly become aware of their resources and are anxious to share them. Others, more timid, less confident, or more abused, may become horrified, terrified or positively aggressive. It takes a while to be able to see that being bereaved, being a refugee, speaking a foreign language, being a mother, having a different ethnic background from the majority, being a housewife, having worked for twenty years as a teacher, are all resources, as are high energy, being able to teach karate and possessing a sense of humour.

In order to be able to see that their varied life and work experiences provide resources, students need to be able to value and understand themselves. Therapeutic work on the course brings increased self-awareness. They learn how to use this helpfully for themselves and others.

It may be necessary for the staff, at first, to show people how to use their own resources. They may do this by self-disclosure used in demonstration counselling sessions or through their personal involvement with the students in tutorials, supervision, feedback on written work or tape recordings. However, the aim is to produce people who are able to recognize their own worth and are able to monitor and assess their own skills and abilities. Rather than assess the students' work the staff will want to monitor and evaluate the students' self assessment and encourage them to develop the skills of monitoring, evaluating and assessing for themselves (see Chapter 2).

Students will also want to use the resources of the staff, the college and each other. The staff make sure that clear information about these is available. There should be a bank of hand-outs clearly catalogued, a helpful librarian who will provide easy access to relevant teaching and learning materials, suggestions for useful workplace visits, suggestions for experiments to aid learning, access to the work of past students, including their learning contracts, use of feedback sheets, visits from people in the community who could have useful information to offer. The students' task now is that of becoming assertive enough to organize resources to meet needs and skilful enough to cope with the feelings of loss when it is realized that not all needs can be met. For example, there may be neither the time nor the staff resources within the group to run a series of workshops on Rogers and behavioural methods in counselling simultaneously. Because the students are now able to express and acknowledge real needs, they may now have the irrational belief that all needs will be met. This of course will not be the case, although if there is a wish and determination to have something it can often be arranged. For example, a student-run workshop on the work of Rogers may be held before the course officially starts for the day, or people may pool information on day or weekend workshops that are being held elsewhere on relevant topics. However, it is unlikely that everyone's needs will be met and the group will have to handle the disappointment and anger of some of its members.

Some knowledge of the way groups work, how to negotiate within them as well as how to handle useful and destructive competitiveness, will be helpful in dealing with the strong swings of emotion that arise in response to unmet needs.

Learning to work in groups

The students must learn to work together. They require the skills of working co-operatively in large and small groups and of surviving as an individual in a community where a great deal of time is spent in groups. The staff offer support in a way that reinforces and extends the students' skills. They hold back from a leadership role and invite the students to take on some of that function. They do not rescue them when they fail but invite them to learn from this. Individuals take time to work out what they can learn. Gradually they create a system where enough people can get enough of their needs met enough of the time.

This involves some maintenance work so that people feel cared about and can care about themselves. At first the staff will maintain the group by using interventions such as the following:

- they offer respect
- they express feelings
- they give information
- they use metaphors or images
- they remember past times or other comparable situations
- they speak straightforwardly
- they make a guess about what people might be thinking or feeling but not saying
- they use basic counselling skills
- they comment on the group dynamics and offer theoretical models.

The staff do not always facilitate, and when they decide to hold back, students find themselves taking more responsibility and trying out new roles. This allows the opportunity for people to try out different roles for themselves. The habitual joker may try out being the one who focuses the group most conscientiously on its task. The nurturer may become the energizer. There will be bids for leadership among the students and hidden rules about who can be allowed to do this unchallenged. People can become characterized in a particular way, for example as 'feelers'. Certain people can become targets. These are situations which, on a counselling course, cannot be ignored or left. If someone is being used as a target or scapegoat this must be straightforwardly acknowledged. People should notice how often it happens, who are the protagonists, what this may be diverting attention from, how people feel about it, whether everyone perceives the situation the same way, the emotional effect on others of this kind of behaviour within the group. If these situations are noticed, course members will be able to see that they are able to collude in the unjust treatment of another and will become more sensitive to the ways this can happen in a wider context. These are occasions to use skilful feedback (see Chapter 2, pp. 14–17), to acknowledge the inevitable competitiveness in the course group and to be prepared to be open about inequality of opportunity within the group.

It will be useful to refer back to agreed guidelines or ground rules concerning fundamental concerns such as confidentiality, use of language, attitudes to oppression, punctuality and a number of other matters which affect the efficient functioning of the learning group. These ground rules are there as a safety net and to allow people to challenge each other within humane boundaries. Without these the course appears to lack structure and it can appear that there is nowhere to go with feelings of extreme distress and helplessness. This means that the student receives clear assistance from the staff in order to achieve her own goals and develop her capacity to work with others to create a productive learning environment. The exercises and ideas listed below have been found helpful in encouraging students to work together to support their learning.

1   Many students find that their learning needs cannot be adequately met without having specific support for their learning. The kind and type of support may vary greatly from one student group to another. For example, a woman student may feel that she cannot be facilitated by a male member of staff over a particular concern. The background to such concerns should be respected and attention given to the difficulties involved. Students generally form small groups to which they bring their concerns. These groups may remain fixed for the duration of the course and can be facilitated by a staff member, or be student-led with consultation from staff. The small home groups or personal development groups generally offer peer support over personal and learning difficulties and are a safe place to debrief after tough sessions.

2   Support should be available also for people who come from social groupings which commonly experience negative discrimination. This support can take the form of a sharpened awareness on the part of white staff regarding the possi-

bility of contributions from a black member of staff being undermined or ignored. This awareness should be followed up by an affirmative response to the black student as well as clearly pointing out what has been happening. Perhaps the most important support that can be given is the visible presence of members of those groups in the staff team. No counselling course can provide a safe haven from racism, sexism or heterosexism, but students must be able to see that both the staff and students are actively working to combat these forces. (See also Chapter 3, pp. 43–6.)

3 Receiving acknowledgement, support and modelling from the staff becomes an important aspect of learning for some. They are eager for workshops delivered by the staff who are still felt to hold important knowledge and expertise. Others will wish to try out their skills away from the staff in student-led groups or workshops. They will need to experience their independence or even become rebellious for a while. Moving straight into staff-run workshops can feel too reminiscent of passive forms of learning which have inhibited them in the past.

4 Students record their learning objectives and describe how these are met or changed over time.

5 Students keep a course journal (which may ultimately form part of the portfolio: see Chapter 2, pp. 29–31). The journal will contain a record of cognitive and affective learning experiences.

6 Students are encouraged to list their strengths and receive feedback on these from others. Because these exercises can be draining and put people in touch with times in their lives when they have been undervalued, it is important to allow people to retain their self-confidence and sense of fun. Asking people to list at least 70 good things about themselves and boast about them to someone else releases energy, laughter and appreciation for themselves and others.

The students will learn to nurture, energize, focus on task, achieve, celebrate and part and be ready to go through the whole cycle again next time they meet. They learn about these phases and the energy that goes with them by being guided through the phases and by slowly, and perhaps unconsciously, acquiring the skills of steering the group themselves.

The students are encouraged to be clear about their starting points: Who am I? Where am I going? What do I want? They are also strengthened by being accepted by others in the light of these. The year ends with a self and peer assessment structure facilitated by the staff. People will have submitted their first audio tape of a piece of counselling which they will have self assessed and they will have had a tutorial with a staff member to discuss their self assessment. They will be encouraged to notice what they have learned and what they want from the rest of the course.

YEAR 2

In the second year the main aim is to ensure that there is a clear working agreement for the whole group, that individual contracts are compatible with this and that the group is beginning to make plans for self and peer assessment.

The tasks and achievements for year 2 are:

- recommitting to the course
- updating learning plans
- clarifying and concretizing a comprehensive working agreement or community contract
- deciding on a plan and appropriate structures for assessment.

Recommitting to the course

The students recommit themselves to the course during a residential weekend where there will be an opportunity to regroup or reform. A small number of students will have left at the end of the foundation year. There may be new course members and new staff. It will be necessary to acknowledge that this is a new group. There will be emotional issues to deal with. People will be reminded of being the 'new girl' at school. They may be feeling abandoned by those who have gone or being intruded upon by newcomers. These feelings about things changing, the sense of loss or abandonment or of being intruded upon, acceptance, inclusion and group membership remind people of developmental events in earlier years and can produce major emotional reactions. People are concerned about identity, their own and the group's, and are reminded of struggling with identity issues within their families, particularly at adolescence. On a self-directed counselling course this restimulation can be used consciously. People may choose to re-enact painful scenarios concerning, for example, the birth of a sibling. They may do this in a small group as part of the planning weekend or later in the year during a workshop on family dynamics or in their personal development groups. There is often a workshop during the weekend on inclusion and exclusion. This is intended to help students look at their emotional investment in including or excluding new people and to become aware of how they may be doing this unconsciously.

The following exercise has been used to help students recognize their feelings about inclusion and exclusion:

Students sit in a tight circle, physically holding on to each other. Other students try to break in while the original circle resists. This goes on for several minutes and understandably breaks through any tendencies to theorize about feeling excluded. People experience being excluding or excluded very forcibly. They are given time to talk about this and encouraged to notice how this could be happening at a less direct level within the group.

This simple exercise has a strong impact and is an example of how a physical and emotional experience complements theoretical understanding.

Students will review what they learned in the foundation year. They realize that they have more knowledge about different counselling models and feel more confident in groups. Students will be expected to do much more for themselves during this weekend than on their first residential. They will be more active at attending to the needs of the group and at providing facilitating structures to accomplish tasks.

Updating learning plans

In the first year students construct a learning plan based on their wants and needs as people and as trainee counsellors or as people who will use counselling skills to enhance other work such as teaching or nursing.

One year on, they will have had an opportunity to assess their new skills, take them back to the workplace, receive feedback from students and staff on their performance in small and large groups, in pairs and triads and on a recording of their work with a client on tape. They will also have received feedback on their ability to monitor their own and others' work. This will have made them aware of a whole new set of strengths and weaknesses as well as different models of counselling in which they could become proficient. They are ready for new understanding and skills through workshops, reading, learning from others, 'happenings' in the large group, applying Kolb's learning cycle to their own styles and constructing their own version of this which is developed out of their learning biography.

During this year the students will start supervision in groups. This brings their work on the course much closer to the work they do with their client group. Supervision brings other learning needs to the fore (see Chapter 6, pp. 92–100).

In the terminology of Egan's three-stage model (Egan, 1990), students will have had the first year to *explore*, now in the second year they take time to digest, integrate and *understand*, while in the third year they will need to consolidate and *act*. The staff using John Heron's three modes of facilitation will gradually abandon the *hierarchical mode*, which may well have been necessary in the first year, and move to a more *co-operative system* in preparation for the third year when they will support the students to be as *autonomous* as possible (see Appendix 2, pp. 107–8.) The students' learning plans will reflect this and might now contain the following items:

I would like to practise facilitating a group following the Tuckman four-stage model (see p. 94).

I would like to learn how to use the current relationship between myself and a client in a more conscious way for therapeutic purposes.

I would like to understand more about transference and how it operates in the large group and between me and my client.

I can envisage using my personal development group, in the first instance, to work on the first item and to use supervision and the large group to work on the second and third items.

The full learning plan should be written down, shown to others, and integrated into the personal contract.

The timetable for the autumn term on the first year of the diploma course may look something like this:

2.00 – 3.00 pm	Weeks 1, 5 and 10 – Community Meeting
	Weeks 2, 3, 4, 6, 7, 8, 9 and 11 – workshops on a variety of topics, such as sexuality, oppression, politics or learning styles.
3.00 – 5.00 pm	Workshops on different models of counselling:
	Gestalt
	psychosynthesis
	psycho-dynamic counselling
	person-centred counselling
5.30 – 7.00 pm	Personal development groups

During this year students are wanting to find their identity as counsellors and will place considerable emphasis on long workshops where they can look at a particular model in depth. In some years groups have opted for ongoing workshops that would last for the full year and cover, for example, a Gestalt approach to counselling. As part of the workshop they would probably do some extensive skills training and practise using the video camera.

Clarifying and concretizing a comprehensive working agreement or Community Contract

Having left the foundation year, the students have also left the nursery slopes. As well as struggles about identity and group membership they have the task of building the diploma course. Course members are concerned to understand what a diploma gained through self-directed learning consists of and means. They may still be uncertain about whether they have constructed the best timetable for themselves. There is likely to be overt and covert resentment towards the staff for not having done it for them. Some students wonder whether a qualification gained in this way will be comparable to other qualifications. The students usually meet the external assessors in this second year and discuss these issues with them. They also spend some time trying to come to grips with what an external assessor does on this type of course. (The role of the external assessors is defined on p. 89.)

During the planning weekend there will have been time to work in depth with some of the concerns raised during the year. Part of the reason for this is to make differences between people clear so that these can be faced and worked with before attempting to draw up a Community Contract.

The course comprises the group of staff and students who are co-operating in the shared enterprise of acquiring counselling skills using a method of self-directed learning. Students need an understanding of the task, and an agreement about what is necessary in order to accomplish it. This is expressed in the Community Contract. It contains the guidelines concerning tasks and roles, recommendations about how to maintain equal opportunities, criteria for assessment, opportunities for evaluation, monitoring, feedback and support, agreements about punctuality and attendance.

The group will also need a formal agreement for its assessment procedure and will show this to the external assessors (see Chapter 2, pp. 26–8).

Deciding on a plan and appropriate structures for assessment

As on any course, assessment is something that should be going on throughout all teaching and learning. If possible there should be a mock assessment at the end of years 1 and 2, and several workshops on assessment should be held so that people learn the necessary skills and accustom themselves to taking on the role of assessor with their peers.

The Community Contract will have outlined the necessary evidence for assessment. Each person then needs an individual contract setting out what they are going to offer as evidence.

The next step is deciding on an assessment procedure, either inventing a new one or using or adapting one that has served in the past (see Chapter 2, pp. 25–9, for a fuller discussion of this, and for a consideration of the pros and cons regarding peer versus staff assessment).

The students work hard to decide how to carry out a just and fair assessment. The topic raises intense fear and anxiety, and self and peer assessment is an extremely challenging task to give a group of students. They work extremely hard to ensure that their assessment is rigorous and thorough.

They discuss a number of issues before finalizing a method that seems satisfactory to all. Some of the questions considered are:

- What is to be assessed?
- How is that to be done?
- What criteria should be used?
- What outcomes are possible?
- What can be done about the different outcomes?
- What is the staff role?
- What is the supervisor's role?

The second year should end with a self and peer assessment procedure run by the students with staff in active attendance as consultants. As in the previous year the students will have produced a piece of self assessed work and discussed this in a tutorial with a member of staff. They will also have taken part in group supervision.

YEAR 3

In year 3 the course group prepares for assessment and carries it out. With the help of individual supervision the students begin to make the transition from working as members of a learning community to working as professionals, using the skills and knowledge they have gained through self-directed learning.

The tasks and achievements for year 3 are:

- recommitment to the course
- updating the learning plan
- finalizing and updating personal and community contracts
- amending and modifying structures and criteria for assessment
- working effectively in the large group
- assessment.

Recommitment to the course

Again the year will start with a residential weekend which allows people to regroup and address important interpersonal concerns. In addition, time is spent looking at how to assess and considering the work to be done in order to complete the course. There is discussion of the task of setting up structures for self and peer assessment, allowing time for this when planning the timetable and for continuing with learning agendas. Students will by now be well used to the idea of self and peer monitoring. Generally in the third year they set up ongoing monitoring groups to prepare for assessment.

The students are now able to work independently as self-directing learners. They can take the knowledge and ideas gained in this rather specialized environment into their professional life.

In addition they are ready for the tasks of self and peer assessment and are thinking of the evidence they will offer and require of satisfactory counselling practice. They will be able to take difficult decisions for clear reasons and according to adequate criteria, and will have found out a great deal about other people's areas of expertise. They will have made arrangements for self and peer monitoring and may be making arrangements for doing this after they have left the course.

Students will have become aware of some of the links between self-directed learning and self-development.

Updating the learning plan

Students will want to consider their learning plan in view of what has and hasn't worked for them over the past two years. Maybe they can see that they would be helped by training or information on how to manage their learning better, that they would be helped by attending workshops on how to assess, that they need help in presenting their portfolio of evidence in an acceptable form. They will negotiate for a timetable designed to accommodate their learning plan.

The timetable for the final year may look like this:

Weeks 1–4	first two weeks only: the whole group meets to decide how and when to assess portfolios and award diplomas, choose monitoring groups and draw up guidelines for them.
Next two weeks	monitoring groups and workshops on a variety of topics (for example, assertiveness, writing contracts, telephone counselling, confronting skills, working within an organization, Transactional Analysis, or assessment).
Week 5	plenary session to confirm contracts.
Weeks 6, 7 and 8	workshops as above.
Week 9	monitoring groups.
Weeks 10, 11 and 12	workshops.
Week 13	evaluation and planning.
5.30 – 7.00 pm each week	personal development groups or monitoring groups.

EXAMPLE OF A WORKSHOP ON ASSESSMENT

1 People work in co-counselling pairs accessing their feelings about the subject.
2 A brainstorm about what areas a good assessment should include.
3 What criteria can be used? Discussion of this in small groups with debriefing in the large group.
4 People consider their strengths and weaknesses as an assessor. They might

put their internal good assessor and bad assessor on a chair and engage in a dialogue between the two. They focus on fears about assessing and may need some time in pairs to consider these further.

5 Finally they are asked to think about what they need in order to be a good assessor. Are they going to be able to get those resources here in the workshop or outside in the large group?

In order to prepare themselves to be assessed, students will want to review their personal contracts. Preferably they should do this in a small group with trusted and challenging colleagues who will ask them to prove that their contract is working and, if it is not, to list some useful additions or models. In the third year they should be able to show how they are taking these ideas into the workplace and using them to find different and innovative ways to fulfil their contract with their employers.

The contract should now be an enabling and useful tool strengthening the student to make action plans and use her skills in interesting new ways. For example, as a result of her experiences of influential interventions in the large group a student counsellor who previously saw her role as counselling distressed students now sees that the organization which houses the students may need to change in order to meet the students' educational and social needs. The counsellor may well think it necessary to work with the structures within the organization rather than solely with the casualties of the system. She will have gained helpful experience on the course by working consciously with others to effect change within the organization for learning that they themselves have created.

By now learners should be able to weigh up the advantages and disadvantages of the self-directed method and have some idea of their progress in using it. They are likely to have become more comfortable with themselves, to be able to be assertive when they choose or use whatever behaviour is necessary to meet their learning needs and help others do the same. Their dependence on staff members will have lessened and they will be able to use them as a reference point rather than a focus. They will have become usefully self-conscious about the way they learn and have a deepened understanding of themselves.

Finalizing and updating personal and community contracts

Having been through at least one trial assessment, students will now be in a position to update their personal contracts and have them in a form that will enable them to be used as the basis for the final assessment and be sent with the completed work to the external assessors. They will use the personal contract to produce a written self assessment and discuss this with their supervisors who may wish to add comments. The personal contract will include a current learning plan and will be compatible with the Community Contract.

The Community Contract may also need to be updated; it should by now be used as a route map containing useful landmarks such as statements about staff and student roles, commitment about time and work and ongoing evaluation, a definition of counselling and a statement about equal opportunities, and assessment procedures and deadlines.

Amending and modifying structures and criteria for assessment

The arrangements for assessment are formal and obligatory. They are created by each community in order to fulfil the relevant part of the formal contract with the college.

A timescale will have to be planned regarding work to be handed in and assessment to take place. This needs to be fitted in with the requirements of the external assessors who see the students' work and return to the course to give feedback. (For an example of an assessment structure, see Chapter 2, pp. 26–7.)

Working effectively in the large group

Many of the tasks in the third year take place in the large group. These meetings tend to be facilitated by the students themselves although the staff are generally there to help with review, feedback and evaluation. It is in the large group that the assessment procedure and timetable are finalized, the Community Contract amended and any queries or problems solved.

These meetings symbolize the shared ownership of the course and as people learn to work well within them they generally become stronger as individuals and clearer about their identity and power. They realize that this is something that must be claimed, rather than given to them. Some people are never comfortable in this forum and find it timewasting or inhibiting. Others find it the most useful part of the course because it offers the possibility of finding and using personal power and, through being alert to the ebb and flow of conflicting feelings, are able to use it to experience themselves more completely.

The staff, particularly in the third year, get out of the students' way so that they can run the large group for themselves. More and more of the meetings are facilitated by the students, with the staff withdrawing to talk about their own concerns. Students are left to overcome their last remaining fears of working in the large group, and a great deal of demonstrable learning takes place. Students learn about themselves through immediate feedback and confrontation, they understand more about how they function in organizations, and work through a number of projections in order to achieve a good method of self and peer assessment.

Assessment

As well as completing their own work for assessment students prepare themselves for the role of assessor. Final structures are decided upon and the requirements for assessees' work clearly communicated (see Chapter 2, pp. 26–7, for an assessment structure). A programme for the assessment day is planned.

The external assessors examine the assessment structures and procedures each year by reading the portfolios of evidence. They comment on the standards of counselling skills that they see in the portfolios and on the changes seen from year to year. They meet the students in small groups and offer feedback about the portfolios. The external assessors also meet with the staff and make comments on the course and its philosophy. They are an important link with other courses and are able to make comparisons with standards reached on different courses. They are practitioners of counselling and therapy and have a strong concern for the service to the clients and for the students' ongoing professional development. They have interested themselves in matters such as the size of the year group, defining the supervisor's role, the appeals system, the allocation of staff time, and preparation for assessment.

The external assessors report to the college authorities and make comments to the staff about any changes that they believe are advisable. This is an opportunity for staff and course development and is valued highly by the staff team.

Awarding the diploma is generally an enjoyable event, with the staff planning a ceremony to enable the students to give the diploma to each other. The course group gathers together for a final time and people then move off to work as self-directing practitioners in a number of different fields. Most students have changed fundamentally. They now see themselves as people with the capacity to meet their own needs through individual and private work and through difficult and invigorating cooperation with others.

This chapter described the tasks necessary to put self-directed learning into action. In the next chapter there is a consideration of the way supervision can be used to support the work on the course and link it to the work with clients.

SIX

Supervision as a support to self-directed learning

Most of this book has been about the everyday life of a learning organization, the philosophy behind it and the challenges it presents. This has necessarily meant depicting and analysing the activities of groups of people, looking at the rationale for the ways in which they work and seeing how they manage their dilemmas.

Supervision focuses on the individual and her professional role and aims to enhance her performance within that role. It does this by helping her establish professional norms and values that are congruent with those of other counsellors, and increase her skills and theoretical knowledge; and by offering support and acknowledgement for difficult and draining work. Supervision in self-directed learning is not different from supervision on other training courses and it fulfils all the usual functions of establishing supporting and enhancing professional practice. On a self-directed training course, however, there should be a strong emphasis on the student's ability to manage her own learning within the supervision, to contract for what she wants and take responsibility for getting her needs met.

Supervision on a self-directed course is complementary and supplementary to the learning on the course itself. In particular it allows learning needs partly addressed on the course to be fully addressed and personalized. It provides a further opportunity for self-direction and offers a safe place for people to practise being self-directing in a pair or in a small supervision group. Supervision allows the student to tease out ways in which her experience of self-direction can be put into practice in her work setting and elsewhere. In this case supervision is acting as a bridge and a monitoring opportunity. It also gives the student a place where she can reflect on her work and monitor and self-assess her performance there.

The primary purpose of all supervision must be to improve the counsellor's performance with the client. When it is supporting self-directed learning the focus will be mainly on how self-directed learning is being put into practice and how this relates to the counselling model in use.

ROLE OF THE SUPERVISOR

Supervision is an enormous help to practising counsellors. The supervisor overlooks but does not oversee her supervisee's caseload. She will receive a great deal of intimate and important information concerning the counsellor's work. It will be as though she is brought into the counselling room. She will have an image of the client, be able to 'hear' her, feel some of the things she feels. Her role is not a managerial one but she may be seen as a refuge, port in a storm, challenger, developer, consultant and colleague. The supervisor on a self-directed course performs most or all of these functions.

Supervision has a major role to play in the two years of the diploma course. Sometimes it seems to be there to fill all the gaps in a necessarily unstructured, loosely defined course curriculum. The supervisor often finds herself spending a large part of the allotted time helping the student make sense for herself of some of the confusing situations that occur.

It is helpful if supervisors also work as members of staff teams or, if not, are practising counsellors who have a good working understanding of self-directed learning in a counselling context. They are there to expand and reinforce what the students learn during college hours as well as to function as supervisors in the normally understood way. There is no advice or problem-solving *for* the student; instead she is offered the opportunity to reflect on the effect the course has had on her personal growth and learning.

The supervisor works to understand the student and to help her understand herself. She helps her explore what she has learned and to begin to plan how she can apply that to the work with clients.

GROUP AND INDIVIDUAL SUPERVISION

When courses were more generously resourced, students might receive over 30 hours of individual supervision in their final year. This was changed to an hour and a half a fortnight of group supervision in the first diploma year with sixteen hours a year individual supervision in the final year. The change came about partly for economic reasons. However, the introduction of group supervision was seen to have many benefits. An important advantage was that it offered the possibility of peer supervision in groups of six or seven people who had a broad spectrum of professional experience to offer. One of the losses was the extensive amount of individual supervision which had provided a valuable counterpoint to the strong emphasis on group work on a normal course day. Supervision is in addition to the normal college day of five hours.

Group and individual supervision support self-directed learning differently. Both, in their different ways, pin down the learning on the course and ask how it can be used. Students can begin to ground the learning and connect it to their personal development and changed ways of behaving. They can be led to see its relevance in the outside world of work, with individual clients, families and organizations.

Group supervision

The group supervisor has the task of bringing many levels of understanding together. Each person in the group can learn from the others. Each member of the group will be at a different stage in her understanding of what counselling is about. Some will still be seeking very direct advice about how to help people better. At the opposite end of the spectrum others will be reflecting on the nuances of parallel processing occurring in the group. In a well-functioning supervision group, students will learn to hear each other better, reflect back, challenge, confront, offer helpful examples from their own experience and suggest theoretical models. The staff member sets an example of this as well as facilitating the group and using the group life as teaching material. She will also share her professional experience and highlight central issues. In addition she will ask the students to decide how, within the parameters of supervision, they want to use the group.

Students can become over-enamoured of group supervision because it has a clear task and structure. It lends itself to very specific exercises and role plays. It is comparatively easy to assess what is learned within group supervision. This is in contrast to planning and working within the main course itself, where people can be swept up by vast waves of feelings and massive experiences which are not always processed and made use of at the time. These are sometimes brought back into supervision and the group supervisor may help the student make sense of particular happenings and link them to things which are pertinent to her clients, for example, feeling isolated, use and abuse of power. However, it is necessary to maintain a delicate balance between helping people make sense of the large group and doing work in group supervision which belongs to the large group itself.

The task is to help students get in touch with creativity, which may be blocked in a larger arena where nobody dares to get up and suggest or try out a solution. They should then be in a position to resume being creative in the large group.

EXAMPLE OF THE USE OF GROUP SUPERVISION

The problem could be something like: 'We aren't heard in the large group. Other people get their needs met but nobody takes any notice of us.' In the small supervision group the students may make a human sculpture of the large group, with particular people putting themselves in a position where they feel powerless. For example, they may sit underneath the chair of someone whom they perceive as more powerful than they are. They can then try moving around and persuading others to move. Gradually they learn to experiment experiencing individual empowerment within a group setting. They realize that they don't all have to do the same thing. The work by the supervision group demonstrates that it is possible to experiment, practise, and eventually change behaviour. Students become more effective and personally empowering in the main course group and elsewhere. The staff member may suggest and facilitate the exercise mentioned above or one or two students may suggest a suitable exercise and take the opportunity to try out their facilitative skills and receive feedback.

Evaluation can be very explicit in group supervision. At the end of a term's work a group can use a simple exercise, for example:

- making a list of the things that worked well
- making individual lists of what each person could do better next term
- deciding what each would have liked to have done more of, or more skilfully
- asking for specific kinds of support or challenge within the group
- asking for specific theoretical input or skill modelling from the facilitator or a student member of the group.

Evaluation will be helped by a clear group contract made in the early stages.

EXAMPLE OF A GROUP SUPERVISION CONTRACT

We want a confidential safe environment in which we can give support, feedback and challenge.

We expect to listen and contribute to the group in an honest and non-judgemental way.

We want other group members to be accepting of our needs.

We want consultation, encouragement and guidance from our facilitator. In particular we would like guidance on working with newly bereaved people. We would like to gain this help by bringing our own client material to the group and using role play to help understand them better.

We want to know more about how groups work through working together and giving feedback and reviewing that process.

Group supervisors will help the group members to come to a useful contract by asking questions such as:

- What do you want to learn in this group?
- How do you want to learn it?

- Who/what will help you?
- What might hinder you?
- What might you do differently by the end of the group?

The group may well spend a whole session constructing its contract so that it can be sure to offer a learning environment that will be facilitative of people's individual ways of learning.

By making a contract with her supervisor the student can prepare herself for using formal or informal contracts with her clients. The contract offers a means of reviewing the way the group or individual sessions are working and provides a means of changing them if necessary. Supervisors will help students form a contract that is going to be helpful to them.

Supervision groups provide an opportunity to study the way groups work. Students can notice how their particular group develops and apply models such as Tuckman's (Tuckman, 1965). Using this model, which suggests that confusion and conflict in the early stages will, if successfully managed, lead to successful performance of the task, the students can become tolerant and skilful regarding differences and difficulties in the early phase and help guide the group to perform well. This additional level of learning within a supervision group may have to be negotiated for, as some group members may want to focus on clients. In reaching a decision the students will again be working to direct their learning in a particular setting and also engaging with the dynamics of the group in order to do so.

The phenomena that occur in the large group are all relevant to the counselling relationship. Chaos, tensions, bids for power, inclusion and exclusion are the experiences of life itself and are rarely missing in the material that a client brings to counselling. In the large group these phenomena can be experienced within the boundaries of the course structure. The supervision group provides a place where these wider and wilder feelings can be examined and reflected upon. Rather than saying that the large group is a frightening place and leaving the fears outside the supervision group, the student can be encouraged to notice who, in this smaller group which is composed of people from the larger group, frightens her, and is invited to explore that in the group. This is usually illuminating and the student becomes aware of how she may create threatening situations by projection and retroflections. In the smaller group she can practise taking back projections and begin to understand how she may punish herself rather than be usefully angry with someone else. She can complete her cycle of experience, reowning projections and returning anger to its source. This will prepare her to work with clients in the same way and to encourage her clients' development so that they too become aware of the ways in which they project difficult feelings onto other people or punish themselves rather than be usefully angry with someone who has hurt them. The time, energy and skills that are devoted to arriving at a compromise or solution will be a measure of the group members' commitment to their own and each other's self-direction.

In the supervision group there can be some stocktaking. Some of the deeper and more traumatic experiences of the large group can be examined and assessed and put into perspective. There will be time for the supervisor to remind the students of the essential ingredients of good counselling and good learning: Rogers' core conditions of warmth, empathy and genuineness. Are these conditions present in the supervision group? Can they be transferred to the more testing conditions of the larger course group? Can the students show that they have the skills to put these conditions into place? How is this being done in the supervision group? How can it be done better?

Individual supervision

This consists of working one-to-one with a chosen supervisor for a contracted number of hours. This should work out at approximately once a fortnight in the final year of a course.

Like the group supervisor, the individual supervisor can be called upon to help the student make sense of difficult situations in the large group. She can use her particular position and her access to the student to help her strengthen herself as a self-directing learner.

EXAMPLE OF AN EXERCISE USED TO SUPPORT SELF-DIRECTED
LEARNING IN INDIVIDUAL SUPERVISION

A normally articulate student talks about feeling completely inhibited and unable to make any contribution when certain individuals appear to be taking over the group. After some discussion and possibly some counselling in connection with this, the supervisor takes the student into the room where these interactions took place. The student is asked to imagine that the individuals are in the room, in their habitual places. The supervisor asks the student to be aware of thoughts, feelings, bodily sensations, etc. and then asks her what she wants to do or say to these people. What does she need to do or say in order to be more self-managing and self-directing in their presence? She may enact speaking to one of these people (played by the supervisor). Speaking to the frightening individuals in this imaginary way helps the student regain her power and her ability to take her rightful place within the learning organization. She may never say these things to the individuals concerned, nor is it necessary for her to do so. Within the exercise she may take on the role of one of these individuals and speak to herself on an empty chair. In this way she confronts her fears and possible projections on to others. This kind of exercise allows a student to complete an experience and free herself from disabling distress. She now feels freer to do and say what she wants.

Students are usually pleased to find themselves with an individual supervisor. It is often a relief from the constant group work. It is also potentially intimidating as it can be scary, intimate and intense. It is less easy to hide in a pair than in a group. Individual supervision is a place for honing skills, deepening awareness, attending to personal development, increasing academic knowledge and receiving individual coaching. It provides the opportunity to experience a one-to-one relationship which has parallels as well as differences with that experienced in one-to-one counselling.

The students receive individual supervision at a time when they are setting up procedures for their final assessment. The supervisor represents the link with the outside world, with the work, with the clients. Either implicitly or explicitly she increases the impetus for providing reliable assessment procedure. The clients must receive a reasonable standard of service. While no two counsellors will work in exactly the same way, there must be common elements in the counselling they receive. These should be guaranteed by the minimum criteria laid down in the Community Contract. Supervisors are likely to want to exert some influence here, encouraging students to think about helpful criteria: for example, 'Students should have a good working knowledge of at least one theoretical model of counselling and demonstrate how they make use of this in their practice' and 'Students should be able to demonstrate that they can judge when to refer a client on for different help'. They will encourage students to develop an individual style of counselling while ensuring that they work within basic common norms and values which are essential to the work with the client.

Students can be given help and support with the work they are producing for assessment. Supervisors will be called upon to offer a great deal of support during self and peer assessment. Students can go back to their supervisor with their difficulties and receive mentoring at a time when there is likely to be some regression, feelings of fear and lack of confidence. They learn something about supervision itself, how to set up a contract, how to choose a supervisor, and begin to think about how they will supervise when they reach that stage.

EXAMPLE OF AN INDIVIDUAL SUPERVISION CONTRACT

My aim is to continue to develop my skills as a counsellor. I want to feel more confident about my skills and abilities. I believe that the more confident I become the more open I will be to feedback and challenge and therefore more able to develop through self-awareness.

To this end I contract

1 To meet twice a month at a particular time and place and to review the work done once a term.
2 To explore the personal meaning of my work, bringing issues from my agency

and from the course as starting points of the session, ending with a decision about action in my personal and professional life.

3   Be aware of my tendency to respond spontaneously from the unconscious and concentrate on developing my observation and reflective skills.

4   Be proactive in the supervision process and spend some time before each session preparing or considering the issues that I want to discuss. I will also expect to identify some area to which I will want to give attention in between supervision sessions.

5   Be open to challenge and feedback and reflect on the content and process of supervision.

I want and expect my supervisor to:

1   Offer a safe place to explore and express my personal feelings – respecting the confidentiality of my work.

2   Offer a consultancy supervision with the emphasis on the educative and supportive function, which will enable me to:

● reflect on the content and process of the counselling and group work I do;
● clarify my thinking, feeling and fantasies;
● develop understanding;
● work with issues from the course, particularly those relating to assessment;
● feel validated, affirmed and challenged in the skills and abilities I already possess.

3   Offer a model which uses immediacy and the supervision relationship as a mirror for my own reactions.

4   Offer a variety of interventions and exercises (e.g. role plays, two-chair work, visualizations) so that I can experience these techniques and feel more confident in using them in my supervision work.

5   Help me to reflect on what the self-directed model of counselling training means to me.

Because individual supervision is experienced towards the end of a course it can provide an opportunity to look at the whole picture of self-directed learning in counselling training. Supervision can provide the student with the opportunity to review her personal perspective, the client's perspective, her perspective as a trainee, a student or as someone who teaches and trains others. Having been helped to consider the course from these different viewpoints she can return to the course group and contribute what she has seen and understood.

Common threads

Group and individual supervision are places to work. Specific examples of what people do with clients in their workplaces are brought and examined. People's attitude to their work will offer evidence of whether the intrinsic meaning of self-direction is being absorbed. Do they set themselves an agenda, notice what they need in order to complete it, look to see if the resources are available, self-monitor and ask for feedback? Or do they wait to be told what to do and when to do it and become angry and anxious if the direction isn't there? Suddenly it becomes evident that, despite appearing to be a powerful, independent, self-directing person, a particular individual is also rather timid when faced with a client or group of clients. She may hope, here in supervision, to be given explicit directions about what to do with a newly bereaved client, for example. The supervisor is more likely, in the first instance, to be more interested in what the student experiences in her client's presence. What does she feel, how does the client feel? What does the supervisee want to do? How does she stop herself doing that? Has she experienced a change within herself which will allow her to trust her inner wisdom, her sense of the situation, her ability to contact the client's inner world? If the supervisor gave all the answers she would be hindering rather than supporting self-direction.

Supervision is there to help a student to stay in touch with her own experience and use that helpfully with another. Self-directed learning forces students to reflect constantly on how they are with another person. The starting point in self-directed learning is the initial contract in which the students agree to take responsibility for their own and others' learning. This encourages them to consider how they can make themselves available usefully to another human being. Each individual, through their good and bad experiences, learns about the function and relevance of the core conditions. Inevitably they will at times experience a lack of listening, being attended to and responded to in the large group. The supervisor helps the student notice that the fundamental conditions for growth and learning are absent and reminds her that she can change this. With this help the student on a self-directed counsellor training course finds out how to alter her environment so that it meets her needs.

The supervisor also endeavours to help the student take full benefit from the opportunities for experiential learning she receives on the course.

For example, the supervisor is often in the position of hearing about and commenting on a number of contentious events, like, for instance, the choosing of small groups. She may explicitly say that this difficult process highlights important happenings in human living, such as choosing or being chosen, being overwhelmed by people or being abandoned by them. She may remind the students that most of us go through life fighting off our feelings and fears about these issues. She asks them to notice how they devote their energy to, for example, avoiding rejection. Most of this exhausting work is secret and some of it is unconscious. Many of the exercises on the course bring out this type of secret. Students need somewhere to go with their exciting and upsetting discoveries. Supervision is a secure place to take these things. Students can be held, contained and respected. As they explore and integrate the personal meaning of events on the course they can be led to feel with their clients, who are generally submerged by their reactions to, for example, grief and mourning, isolation, rejection. On a course where the emphasis is on self-directed and experiential learning such issues are continually being presented. Students cannot avoid their own experience. They learn to accept it. The message is: accept your own experience, be alive to its subjective meaning, accept the help of others and be available and present for them when they need help.

Supervision may occupy a rather private, even split-off space. Sometimes students tell the supervisor what they 'really feel' about things, saying they cannot possibly mention this in the large group or even in small groups or workshops. Supervision could become an idealized space with the supervisor seeming to be the only person who could possibly understand what significance a particular event has for a student. While it is vital for the student to use supervision to explore and clarify, the supervisor should be able to resist the seductive and powerful role of confidante and work catalytically so that the student returns to her peers able to use her knowledge in mainstream areas of the course. Rather than the power and energy staying within the private relationship with the supervisor the student can enrich the course by returning to the group and contributing her increased understanding.

This involves both supervisor and student in thinking about the course as an interconnecting set of processes: workshops, small groups, large group, supervision, staff teams and staff meetings. The hope is that the student will be able to use supervision to review her response in the course group. She is then likely to be able to go back capable of acting differently and more autonomously. The supervisor helps the student to examine the relationship within the supervision pair or group, and then to look outwards toward the work and back towards the course.

If the supervisor is working well within the staff team she will have a good idea of important issues on the course, what the hold-ups are and the areas of most contention. These issues will surface in some way in supervision. The supervisor should be able to offer some fresh perspectives and, if necessary, confront the student, perhaps with the way she is handling a similar issue within supervision or with things that she is avoiding. In order to be able to do this well the supervisor should feel herself to be a regular member of the staff team, attending meetings and being part of any policy change.

The supervisor works with students in the following seven ways:

1 She helps students understand how counselling works.
2 She helps students process their experience, i.e. deal with, resolve and integrate the feelings that arise in response to events on the course and work with clients.

3 She offers a transitional space where the student can wait, observe, reflect upon and assess her learning and her ability to be a self-directing counsellor before taking on the role of counsellor in a fully autonomous way.
4 She helps to build a bridge to the work outside the course.
5 She encourages the student to continue developing as a person.
6 She is an essential part of the course team and exerts a direct, visible influence on standards.
7 The supervisor is vigilant in encouraging the student's autonomy and in ensuring that she takes her skills as a self-directing learner out into the working world.

Students approach supervision with anxiety and relief. There is anxiety at the thought of exposing their professional practice and relief at the prospect of some close contact and a nurturing relationship with a self-chosen member of staff. The supervisor is likely to be the recipient of strong positive transference and may be tempted to take on the role of wise woman or simply to offer unlimited supplies of warmth and support. But the role is more complex.

The good supervisor must know when to tip the nest and withdraw protection, let the student be anxious and find her way on her own.

In the words of Clarissa Pinkola Estes (1993), 'she must be both escort and teacher. She is a loving mother but also fierce and demanding.'

SEVEN
Key areas in self-directed learning

This chapter sets out the key aspects of self-directed learning. It describes the contract or working agreement between students and staff and what students do to implement a training of this kind. It then briefly comments on possible distortions of the self-directed learning process, the gains to be expected from this kind of training, and where it can lead.

THE CONTRACT

Students undertake responsibility for their own learning; they agree to work with others and facilitate the learning of others; they agree to self and peer assess in order to award or not to award a diploma to each other; and they contract to do this work within certain boundaries laid down in advance by the staff.

HOW STUDENTS IMPLEMENT SELF-DIRECTION IN COUNSELLING TRAINING

Self-directed learning is successful when both the group and its individual members find direction, fulfil their tasks, become sensitive to process, to the way the tasks are carried out, and acquire new skills and knowledge and a belief in the possibility of change.

Self-directed learning in counselling training requires the students define their needs and focus on them. They become centred on these needs and their shared tasks. They become integrated into a learning group, share skills and personal information with others, learn to support each other and engage in work that is useful to their tasks. As they do this they become able to integrate knowledge and skills. They explore new concepts and ways of relating. They became familiar with further aspects of themselves and find ways of behaving differently and hearing what others make of this. They can now see how some of their buried traumas may have made new learning difficult.

Within small groups and workshops they define and focus what they have learned. They also share their feelings and personal experience. They support each other and orient themselves towards the tasks ahead. They integrate the known and unknown and develop new skills.

DISTORTIONS IN THE SELF-DIRECTED LEARNING PROCESS

Distortions will occur in self-directed learning where there is an over-emphasis on either task or process, or where the power and influence of the group oppress the individual and eventually subvert self-direction. In these situations students do not find direction, they do not fulfil their tasks, and they do not acquire new skills and knowledge. These problems can be alleviated by an understanding of group dynamics and by paying particular attention to the different skills needed at each stage of the course. This is discussed within the text (in particular in Chapter 3); the diagram on p. 107 of Appendix 2 shows some of the skills needed by both students and staff during the different developmental phases of the course.

WHAT STUDENTS GAIN AS PEOPLE AND PRACTITIONERS

Students gain an understanding of how they learn and change. They become able to relate to each other spontaneously and to take responsibility for their own personal development.

As staff work with students in self-directed learning communities they see most of them change quite quickly in a number of ways. Most of the students are aware of these changes and speak of them positively.

There is an increased understanding of how to learn from group dynamics. Students feel different, partly because within the large and smaller groups they become free and open about personal needs. They benefit from being given time and encouragement to reassess previous patterns of learning and from noticing the effect of new and different ways of learning. They notice and celebrate change and understand their responsibility in effecting change. They gain the skills to offer this freedom and responsibility to others. Students also gain an increase in insight and personal awareness and become capable of more productive relationships. They learn more about their own and others' behaviour and how this can enable or disenable learning. They receive a heightened ability to perceive and understand their own process and that of others. They become familiar with the relationship between feeling and responding and learning. They become able to put Rogers' core conditions into practice and become proficient at the skills of attending, responding, disclosing and challenging.

In order to construct and plan a course the students must react to each other spontaneously and straightforwardly. As a result of this they become increasingly aware of how what they say can be facilitative or inhibiting of another. Over time they also see how unconscious processes can interact and affect the life of the group or individual. They realize that such processes will have an impact on learning. As they become aware of how in the past they may have sabotaged themselves, they are able to be much more skilful at putting plans into action and bring them to a successful implementation. They are prepared to take risks to do so. They take an increasing personal responsibility for their own state of being and are willing to be proactive to enhance that state.

They have learned more about their needs and values and how these influence their attitudes, assumptions and judgements. They have learned to think more carefully about how to acquire and use resources and become confident in their ability to create a good enough learning environment.

WHERE THESE ACHIEVEMENTS LEAD

Each new generation of students creates a learning environment from within the structures and restrictions given. The achievement lies in creating an organization for learning which allows its members to direct their own learning as well as directing some of that learning towards themselves. This leaves students with a model of how a learning organization can work and can be responsive to the needs of those within it. They build a community that can adapt to their changing needs and they work within that community to meet their needs.

Students are now able to approach their workplaces as thinking adults wanting to be consulted over the way the organization works. Because they have had to face their negative as well as their positive impulses their experience of self-direction enables their curiosity and desire to learn to overcome their tendencies towards regression. This can have an important effect on organizations, many of which are having to reinvent themselves so as to become more responsive to change. The people working within them will need to know each other and be able to express their shared aspirations. Ideally they will want to build a living community that is sensitive to their changing needs. They require skills and enough goodwill to talk about attitudes and beliefs in a non-polarized way. People across racial and other divides have to find out enough about each other in order to work together. They have the task of constructing effective working relationships and of creating an organization that supports learning.

Consultants are having to discover the forces that help and the forces that hinder change. They can draw the organization's attention to the connections and inter-relationships between people and how these are affected by top-down management decisions. Commenting on and making these connections allows the learning organization to stay in contact with its human resources. It seeks, looks for and works with change. It needs people within it who are themselves able to change and learn new skills, which may be more important than high-level grades or qualifications. If staff can be encouraged to involve themselves in the things that interest them deeply they are likely to contribute positively to an organization. They are engaged in tasks that are personally relevant to them and are therefore highly motivated to achieve them. An organization containing such people achieves a balance between the reluctance for change and the desire to seek and work for it.

Self-directed learning prepares people to be active in the world. Counsellors who are trained using this model will be enabled to support groups and individuals through many different kinds of change and will continue as self-directing learners themselves. At the end of a course of training they can experience closure but also envisage experiences and opportunities for transmitting and transforming the culture they have created.

APPENDIX 1

Alternative timetable for introductory planning weekend

Day 1 (Friday evening)
Welcome. Brief introduction to the course and to the weekend.

People say their names so that everyone has spoken once in the large group.

Exercise 'Luggage Rack': people are asked to imagine leaving their immediate pressing concerns on a luggage rack over their heads. They speak briefly to their neighbour about this experience.

Various kinds of ice-breakers and name games.

The course and the role of self-directed learning is re-explained.

People are put into temporary 'home groups' or counselling triads, with access to a named member of staff as resource person. They are given time in these before convening briefly for a final meeting.

Day 2
Name games.

Time in home groups or triads.

Time is allowed in the main group for people to check in with thoughts, questions, feelings left over from the previous evening.

Working first on their own, then in pairs, then in groups of four or five, people write down their hopes, fears and expectations for the weekend. These are written on flip charts and referred to during the weekend.

There is a guided fantasy about early school experience. People debrief about this in small groups facilitated by tutors.

Time in original home groups or triads.

There is some debriefing in the large group and people are asked to start to think about what they want to learn on the course and how they want to learn it. Tutors give examples, ask questions, give answers.

Day 3
The whole group gathers for an introduction to the day. There is a feedback session and a reminder about names.

The 'Lifeline' exercise (see above, p. 60) is done and time is allowed for debriefing and recovery.

There are small groups with tutors and some discussion about a learning plan. Each person is encouraged to give their ideas so far on this and to have a written plan.

People are encouraged to list some of the things they are good at. Finally, in groups of four or five they arrive at a list of resources. They pin this up on the wall with the tutors working as a small group and doing the same. If the students feel that their learning plans are complete they may be ready to match needs and resources. However it is quite likely that students may become aware of a number of complex issues arising from early childhood and particularly early experiences in education. These considerations will affect their learning needs and they may not be ready to complete a plan or a timetable.

The staff work in the large group to draw issues together and devise a suitable ending that will celebrate the work done and suggest ways to work on what is still undone.

Staff work regularly together in their home group.

A developmental model for student skill building and staff methods of facilitation

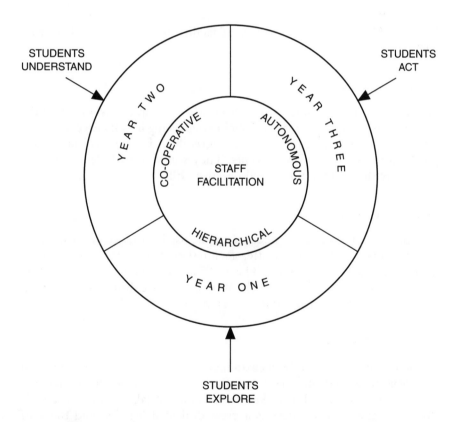

STUDENTS
UNDERSTAND

STUDENTS
ACT

YEAR TWO

YEAR THREE

CO-OPERATIVE

AUTONOMOUS

STAFF
FACILITATION

HIERARCHICAL

YEAR ONE

STUDENTS
EXPLORE

Figure A.1 Developmental model for student skill building (outer circle) and staff methods of facilitation (inner circle)

Egan's three-stage model (Egan, 1990) applied to student skill building over the three years of a course:

YEAR 1 – EXPLORE

In the first year students learn to identify core experiences and themes, they become more familiar with their feelings and start to achieve clarity.

YEAR 2 – UNDERSTAND

In the second year they consider possibilities and agendas. They look at what is involved in making choices and commitments.

YEAR 3 – ACT

In the third year they can evolve strategies and plans and take action.

For the staff, Heron's three modes of facilitation may be useful (Heron, 1989):

YEAR 1 – HIERARCHICAL

Hierarchical facilitation is used early on where it can be assumed that the students do not know a great deal about counselling or self-directed learning. In this stage, if the students are agreeable, the staff will take some power to organize and direct events. They will still work democratically in the way they communicate and practise skills.

YEAR 2 – CO-OPERATIVE

Co-operative methods of facilitation may be used in the second year where the students will be able to offer facilitation themselves and will have gained knowledge and skills. The staff are not in unilateral control. Decisions are made collaboratively. Where there are differences common ground is sought and compromises arrived at.

YEAR 3 – AUTONOMOUS

The students will by now be accustomed to making learning contracts and be engaging in self and peer assessment. It is now assumed that the students have a great deal of knowledge and can take action and decide things for themselves. There is a great deal of delegation and the staff work mainly as consultants.

Bibliography

Berne, Eric (1964) *Games People Play: The Psychology of Human Relations*. New York: Grove Press.

British Association for Counselling (1990) *Code of Ethics and Practice for Counsellors*. Rugby: British Association for Counselling.

Charleton, Mary, Hewitt, Sue and Proctor, Bridget (1987) *South West London Counselling Course Student Manual*. London: South West London College.

Demaré, P. et al. (1991) *Koinonia: From Hate, through Dialogue, to Culture in the Large Group*. London: Karnac.

Egan, Gerard (1990) *The Skilled Helper* (4th edn). Pacific Grove, CA: Brooks Cole.

Estes, Clarissa Pinkola (1993) *Women Who Run with Wolves*. London: Random House.

Evison, R. and Ronaldson, B. (1975) *British Journal of Guidance and Counselling* 3 (1), 82–92.

Gray, Kenneth (1993) *Counsellor Interventions in Organisations*. Careers Research Advisory Council. First published *British Journal of Guidance and Counselling* 12 (1), January 1984.

Heron, John (1974) *The Concept of a Peer Learning Community*. Guildford: Department of Adult Education, University of Surrey.

Heron, John (1977) *Catharsis in Human Development*. London: British Postgraduate Medical Federation, University of London Research Project in association with the Human Potential Research Group.

Heron, John (1986) *Six Category Intervention Analysis* (2nd edn). Guildford: Human Potential Resource Group, University of Surrey.

Heron, John (1989) *The Facilitator's Hand Book*. London: Kogan Page.

Heron, John (1990) *A Handbook for Leaders*. Guildford: Human Potential Resource Group, University of Surrey.

Houston, Gaie (n.d.) On becoming a self-directed course. Internal mimeo, South West London College.

Jackins, Harvey (1973) *The Human Situation*. Seattle: Rational Island Publishers.
Jackins, Harvey (1994) *Co-counselling Manual* (rev. edn). Seattle: Rational Island Publishing.
Kendall, Rosanna (1982) *The Art of Self-managed Learning: A Practical Approach*. London: London Regional Training Unit.
Kilty, James (1978) Design for learning. Paper, British Postgraduate Medical Federation, January.
Kolb, David (1984) *Experimental Learning*. Englewood Cliffs, NJ: Prentice-Hall.
Kreeger, Lionel (ed.) (1975) *The Large Group*. London: Anchor Press.
Mearns, D. and Thorne, B. (1988) *Person-Centred Counselling in Action*. London: Sage.
Perls, Fritz (1972) *Gestalt Therapy* (original US edn 1951). London: Souvenir Press.
Proctor, Bridget (*c.* 1985) *The Individual and the Co-operative Group*. Videotape, in conjunction with Inner London Education Authority.
Proctor, Bridget (1991) On being a trainer. In W. Dryden and B. Thorne (eds), *Training and Supervision for Counselling in Action*. London: Sage.
Rogers, Carl (1961) *On Becoming a Person*. London: Constable.
Rogers, Carl (1994) *Freedom to Learn*. New York: Macmillan.
Satir, Virginia (1972) *Peoplemaking*. Palo Alto, CA: Science and Behavior Books.
Self and Society (1984), whole edition edited by Mary Charleton, *European Journal of Humanistic Psychology* **XII** (4), July/August.
Silverstone, Liesl (1993) *Art Therapy – The Person Centred Way*. London: Autonomy Books.
Tuckman, B. W. (1965) Developmental sequences in small groups. *Psychological Bulletin* **63** (6).
Worrell, Judith and Remer, Pam (1992) *Feminist Perspectives in Therapy*. Chichester: Wiley.

Index